D1570013

WHEN
GOD
Whispers

—Terry Helwig—

BROADMAN PRESS
Nashville, Tennessee

LIBRARY OF CONGRESS
Library of Congress Cataloging-in-Publication Data

Helwig, Terry, 1949-
  When God whispers.
    p. cm.
  ISBN 0-8054-5734-8
  1. Spiritual life I. Title.
BV4501.2.H369564   1988
242—dc19

87-34490
CIP

For My Sisters
Nancy, Vicki, Pattie, Brenda, Joni, and Robin

Acknowledgments

To my loving husband, Jim, whose critiques have brought focus to my thoughts; to my daughter, Mandy, who has become my deepest source of inspiration; and to my family and friends, who have given me enough "alone time" to write . . . I give my thanks and deep affection.

Preface

One night I rested my head upon my husband's chest. In the stillness I heard it. It was his heart, beating quietly, within inches of my ear. I pondered the miracle of the heart, the life-force of every living creature, forever pulsing within us, throbbing moment by moment, day after day, year after year.

When God Whispers is about the times I have placed my ear against the world and heard—coming from within it—the heartbeat of God. When I stand on a mountaintop or watch the sun sink into the ocean, I hear it. I hear it when I look at Mother Teresa, when I hug my daughter, when I wipe a tear of joy from my cheek. I hear it in the darkness, coming from the tomb.

My prayer is that this book will help you in your search to hear God whispering. I offer you my experiences as I would offer you a basket of seashells. Take those that speak to you, the ones with which you can identify. When you press your shell against my ear and I press mine against yours, we both can hear the heartbeat of God, forever pulsing, throughout all creation.

Contents

It is well to stop our star gazing occasionally and consider the ground under our feet. Maybe it is celestial, too; maybe this brown, sun-tanned, sin-stained earth is a sister to the morning and the evening star.

—John Burroughs

1
When God Whispers

Mandy crossed her arms and furrowed her dark brows. "What's the oldest number you can be? You know the *last* number?"

My foot rested on the brake at the intersection. Mandy sat beside me, the top of her head just barely reaching above the window. We were on our way to get ice cream cones. She kept staring at me. She expected an answer. Did I know the last number?

I squirmed. The last number! How do you explain infinity to someone who still believes in Santa Claus? I wished I could say, with absolute authority, "The last number is one hundred trillion, quadrillion million!"

I cleared my throat. "You know this may sound silly, but there is no end number. You could keep on counting forever and ever." I wished I had a better answer. "It's a hard thing to understand," I said.

"I bet God knows the answer," she stated matter-of-factly. "And when I get to heaven, I'm going to ask Him."

Then evidently deciding she could not wait that long, she stuck her pug nose outside the window and shouted: "God, what is the oldest number you can get to be?" Unlike me, she paid no attention to the man in the convertible beside us. Instead, she waited in silence.

I did not know she *really* expected God to answer until she turned toward me. The bridge of her nose wrinkled like a raisin. Her eyes searched mine. "Mommy, why doesn't God talk to me?"

The gulf of silence grew between us. I, too, was a child at that moment. God's child. And as God's child, I have often asked Him the same question. I have waited in the early morning darkness, almost holding my breath, searching for an answer, a sign, any assurance that God has heard me. I have wished that the moonlight coming in through the bedroom window would shimmer and come alive, taking the form of an angel or a message on the wall. I have longed for God to speak to me, to call out my name. I have told myself that maybe if I were to go somewhere—to a mountaintop—to lay beneath the stars and ponder the mysteries of the universe I would hear God, speaking plainly from the heavens, as He spoke to Moses and Abraham.

But how am I to escape the *worldly* things that seem to require my attention, things like: "We're out of towels again!" or "Could you sew this button on for me?" or "Mommy, will you help me look for Barbie's shoe?" I do not think God intends for me to become a hermit or mystic searching the inner sanctums of quietness and solitude for His voice. I do not think I will see an angel made of moonlight. It seems that, if I am to hear God whispering into my life, I will have to do it despite the commotion of a preschooler, a job, a house, a television, and a telephone.

For whatever reason, God has chosen to whisper into my life instead of shout. And this makes my task more difficult. Whispers are easy to ignore; if I am too busy or too distracted, I may never hear a thing. Denying a God whose voice rattles the crystal in the china hutch is hard. Denying a God who whispers in a noisy world is easy. The choice is mine. I can pause and strain to hear what God is trying to tell me, or I can walk away and convince myself that I never heard a thing.

I often think of Helen Keller who was both blind and deaf. Before Helen's patient teacher, Anne Sullivan, came into her life, Helen's communication was primitive and limited. In her biography Helen wrote how difficult it was for her to be "locked up" in another world. She said that her failures to make herself understood were invariably followed by outbursts of passion. In her own words she said,

> I felt as if invisible hands were holding me, and I made frantic efforts to free myself. I struggled—not that struggling helped matters, . . . I generally broke down in tears and physical exhaustion. If my mother happened to be near I crept into her arms, too miserable even to remember the cause of the tempest. After awhile the need of some means of communication became so urgent that these outbursts occurred daily, sometimes hourly.[1]

When Anne pumped water onto Helen's palm and repeatedly spelled w-a-t-e-r, Helen awakened to the mystery of language. She said that suddenly she felt a misty consciousness of something forgotten—a thrill of returning thought. She understood that the symbols being pressed upon her hand described the wonderful cool something that was flowing over her fingertips. It was as if the water became a "living word"[2] that awakened her soul, gave it light, hope, joy, and set it free! At long last Helen had found a way out of her darkness.

I think we are all Helen Kellers. We find ourselves born into this world with eyes and ears incapable of seeing and hearing God's world. We are handicapped from birth. God, understanding our limitations, tries to find another way to communicate. He reaches out and touches us in some way.

At first the touches may seem random and have no meaning. But one day, beneath the water pump, with cool water tickling our fingertips, we hear a whisper in our minds. A misty consciousness of something forgotten turns into awareness. And we know we have been touched differently. The timing of the touch *means* something. God has spoken. Perhaps we realize, for the first time, that the God without is forever whispering to the God within.

Can you imagine the joy, the singing of heavenly angels, when a child of God has finally made that connection? The joy must mirror that of Helen as she ran into her parents' arms. She had been touched in such a way that she would never be the same again.

Learning to Recognize God's Whisper

Like Helen, I am sometimes engulfed in darkness—emotional darkness. At these times I feel that I am looking at God through the small end of a periscope. He appears to be very, very far away, so far away that I cannot begin to hear what He has to say to me. In fact, when I was thirteen, I thought He had disappeared altogether.

I remember a particular night when I waited for my younger sister to fall asleep beside me. Moonlight spilled through our small trailer-house window. And Boots, my scarred tom cat, purred beside me. I hugged him and drew him so close that I could feel his heartbeat beneath his warm fur. I clung to him in order that I might not drown.

My tears left long dark streaks on Boot's fur. He did not seem to mind. He seemed to know I needed him. I could not tell anyone why I was crying, not even Daddy. Mama had made me promise not to tell. I had no one to talk to—except Boots. So there in the cold shadows of darkness, I released my tourniquet of silence, and the words came gushing forth like blood from a wound.

"Mama is dying, Boots. She only has two more years to

live. What will I do without her? I'm the oldest. I have to be strong for my sisters. But I don't know if I can go on without her. Oh, it hurts so much, Boots. It hurts so much."

Boots purred and rubbed his head against my palm. His ragged ear, part of which was torn away in a cat fight long ago, nuzzled against my flesh. The thought of Mama's death ripped through me. If my heart ever healed, I knew it would be ragged and torn like Boots's left ear.

In that year, I watched for symptoms of Mama's disease. I waited. I prayed for her. And almost every night, after my sisters had fallen asleep, I cried. And always it seemed Boots was there: purring, listening, and comforting.

It's odd. I can remember the night Mama told me she would die, but I cannot remember how I learned she would live. Maybe it was the passing of time, the lack of symptoms, or the realization that Mama had another problem. An emotional illness would haunt her off and on throughout her life. Mama was not really dying, at least not in the physical sense. She only believed she was dying. I was relieved, certainly. But I had these scars on the inside, ugly and misshapen, where scalding tears had burned their way out of me.

Reconciling this period of my life into my faith has been difficult for me. Where was God in all of this? I ask. If I believe God is forever whispering in my life, where was He and what was He saying?

Part of my answer came in a poem called "Footprints." The author is anonymous, his name separated from his poem, but his words illumine such a truth that they live on and on.

The poem is about a man looking at the footprints of his life upon the sand. When he sees two sets of footprints, he knows the Lord has been walking with him. But he is troubled when he sees only one set of footprints in the sand during the most difficult periods in his life.

He asks in disbelief. "Why, during the most difficult times in my life, Lord, did You leave me to walk all alone?"

But the Lord reassures him. "My son, when you see only one set of footprints in the sand, that is when I carried you."

Could it be that the one set of footprints upon my thirteenth year belonged to my Heavenly Father and not to me? Could it be that God carried me when I thought I was walking alone? When I pause and strain, I hear a whisper deep within me. It's as if God is saying: "My precious child, I do not cause pain. But I am always present in pain. I have never deserted you. Even in the darkest moments of your life, I have been there . . . whispering.

"When you were thirteen, maybe you did not recognize Me. I wiped your tears with the fur of an old tom cat named Boots. It was I who gave you to each other."

And, looking back, I see God has always been whispering, making symbols in the palm of my hand, hoping one day I would make the connection—that His whispers and the symbols are related to one another. He asks only that I become conscious as He tries to awaken that image of Himself within me. What He wants most is for me to become aware that He is not as silent as I often believe Him to be.

How about you? Do you long to hear God whispering into your life? Is it possible that God, right at this moment, is making symbols in the palm of your hand? Is He trying to tell you something? Has He carried you in the arms of your aunt or your grandfather? Or has He whispered His love through something even more unlikely, like an old tom cat named Boots?

Listening for God

I think of Elijah as he stood upon the mountain before the Lord. First Kings 19:2-15 says that a great and powerful wind tore apart the mountains and shattered the rocks but the Lord was not in the wind. After the wind came an earthquake, but the Lord was not in the earthquake. After the earthquake came a fire, but the Lord was not in the fire. After the fire came a still small voice, a whisper. God whispered to Elijah.

God whispers to all of us. Oh, His voice may not vibrate against our eardrums, but we receive a message within us. It comes as tinkling, a knowing, a still, small voice that confirms. We do not need eyes or ears to recognize God.

I realized that after learning of another young girl born both blind and deaf. No one had ever told her about God before. Then one day, with touch signs on the palm of her hand, someone tried to explain Him. As she "listened," her face lit up. She excitedly signaled back: "God! Is that what you call Him? I have known Him a long time, but I never knew His name."

Whether we know His name, whether we choose to listen, God gives evidence of Himself through all creation. We cannot deny His presence anymore than we can pull down a shade and say: "There! The sun is no longer shining."

So, when my daughter asked in the car that afternoon, "Why doesn't God talk to me?" I could not deny that God had just whispered to me through her. I believe her question was an answer to my prayer.

Earlier that morning, sitting at my desk, I had buried my head in my arms—a sure sign of defeat. Sometimes writing is like that. It comes hard. For days, I had shuffled papers and ideas looking for just the right beginning. Just the right message. My prayer was earnest: "Lord, I believe You whisper. I want to share that belief. Please whisper to me today. Show me where to begin."

That very afternoon my daughter talked about hearing God for the first time in her life. When things like that happen, I get goose bumps all the way to the top of my head. I feel that familiar tinkling inside, that confirming feeling that draws me closer to my Creator. I found myself telling my daughter that God does *talk* to us, but not like we talk to each other.

Oh, my logical nature tries to pull down the shade and deny the experience. *Whispers from God? Don't be silly! Coincidence. That's all it is.*

But again I think of Anne, repeatedly, pressing her fingers into Helen's palm. She hoped that somewhere deep inside, Helen might hear a still, small voice whispering, *There is a pattern. There is a meaning. You are on the threshold of discovering a new way to communicate.* Then Helen had to do what each of us has to do after we have heard the still, small voice inside us. We have to trust what it says.

Trusting the Still, Small Voice

The still, small voice comes with a very high price tag. Sometimes I have been unwilling to pay the cost. For you see, I have to trust, and trusting is hard for me. I am afraid I will be let down or made a fool. I have often wished I were as trusting as Noah. Noah paid the price. How else could he shoulder the laughter as he fashioned gopher wood into an ark? But I sometimes wonder, in the stillness of morning, if Noah ever doubted what he heard?

Doubt is paralyzing. I am reminded, through the story of a young boy, how life threatening doubt can become. A young boy stood on a window ledge two stories high, waging a war of trust. Tongues of fire threatened to devour him. His frantic father called again from below. "Son, you have to jump!"

The boy doubted. Jump? Into the heat and choking black clouds? Surely his father had not told him to jump.

"Daddy, I can't see you," he cried.

"I know," his father reassured, "But I can see you!"

So the boy trusted. He took a deep breath and jumped. He fell through what must have seemed like hell and landed safely in his father's arms.

I wonder how many times I have turned my back because I was afraid to jump? How many times have I assumed that the symbols pressed into the palm of my hand held no meaning? How many times have I walked away from a whispering God only to bulldoze through my day, camouflaging His message with the noises of my world, like a child blowing incessantly on a whistle?

I am discovering something. When I put down my whistle, I hear the faint tinkling within me, the whisper, the knowledge that God is beside me. And as I listen to God call me, I take a deep breath and jump. The fall into His arms is scary. It requires trust because I could, after all, be made a fool. What kind of person believes that an old tom cat and a child's question at a traffic light are whispers from God?

Somehow I feel like the boy on the window ledge— doubting, wondering, and yet knowing. I have to trust. My very life depends upon it.

Notes

1. Helen Keller, *The Story of My Life* (Garden City, N.Y.: Doubleday & Company, Inc., 1905), p. 32.
2. Ibid., p. 36.

This is my Father's world,
And to my list'ning ears
All nature sings, and round me rings
The music of the spheres.

This is my Father's world,
I rest me in the thought
Of rocks and trees, of skies and seas;
His hand the wonders wrought.

—Maltbie D. Babcock

2
Does God Really Whisper?

Jesus promised, "I am with you alway, even unto the end of the world" (Matt. 28:20).

I believe Jesus meant it when He said He is with us always! Even our doubts cannot separate us. In *Agony of Christianity,* Miguel de Unamuno wrote, "Faith which does not doubt is dead faith." A doubting faith may be more desirable than one which passively accepts ritual and traditions. I don't think it is any accident that one of the disciples, Thomas, doubted Jesus. I think within each of us is a "doubting Thomas." We may have to "prove" to our Thomas, like Jesus did, the many ways that God whispers into our lives.

Faith has not come easily for me. I have not only doubted like Thomas but have often felt like Peter as I raise my foot over the edge of the boat. In my doubt, I never know for sure if I am stepping *into* or *onto* the water. Will I sink beneath the surface as I step out in faith? Or will I walk? In this instance, walking means hearing God whisper into my life. It means believing God guides me. It means believing God has a limitless capacity to communicate with His children, even though we are narrow creatures of logic and scientific data.

Imagine asking a scientist to evaluate a beautiful painting. After extensive tests he could probably determine the kinds and colors of paints used and the type of surface

25

on which the painting was painted. Perhaps, he could even date the painting and suggest what kinds of brushes and strokes were used. But not one of his tests could determine for certain *who* painted the painting.

That is the dilemma we all face. We can determine the kinds and colors of paints used in our lives. We can even identify the type of surface on which our lives are painted. But when it comes to proving who brought the canvas and the paints together, we have no proof. How do you prove who is the artist unless you watched him paint the painting? And if we do not see him, do we then say no artist exists because we cannot name him?

Each of us has to determine if we believe God is the artist of our lives. And as such, does He *really* whisper. Perhaps it helps to reflect upon our lives. Have we felt God's presence? Have we received confirmation through circumstances or someone else? Have we felt a nudging to do something? Have we experienced unexplainable coincidences? Do these things occur randomly? Or is it possible our Creator dips His brush into our existence? Could it be each stroke of the paintbrush is a whisper from God?

Scientific tests and narrow logic are of little value as I struggle to hear God in my noisy world. Faith seems to be my greatest asset. Faith tells me that every painting requires an artist. Faith tells me that our existence has rhyme and reason. Faith tells me that a loving Father bends and whispers His love and guidance to all who will listen.

God Whispers in Between the Static

Listening for God's voice in a noisy world may parallel trying to hear a radio broadcast interrupted by static. I remember my grandfather, hunched over a crackling radio, straining to listen to a newscast. The static hissed and popped and, at times, drowned out the announcer. The more frequent and longer the static became, the less the announcer could be understood.

Like a buzzing bee, our busyness may produce static. The louder we buzz, the harder it is to hear. If our minds are constantly in a state of motion, like the stirred-up bottom of a river bed, it is very possible that we are sending up a spiritual busy signal to God. In essence, we say: *I'm sorry, God, I don't have time to listen to you right now. I'm busy . . . so busy. Maybe later, when I have more time.*

Instead of hearing God whisper throughout the day, I sometimes allow the static of my life to override the importance of communion with Him. When I tune God out, I become like the outer-space puppets I saw on a television program my daughter watches. Disgruntled, they flip the radio dial from every clear channel. Finally, they find what they were looking for—static.

When I forget God, I, too, am listening to static only. Becoming conscious of God in busy moments is often a struggle. But then I picture my grandfather, hunched over the radio, listening despite the static. It may be hard to hear God's whisper in a noisy world. But if we draw close, our chances of hearing Him are greater.

I have to struggle to bring this listening into the hectic pace of my life. I too easily fall into the trap of what I call *surface living*—merely existing from day to day, without giving thought to a personal relationship with God. Numerous times I am pierced with the thought of how long it has been since I last listened for His voice.

Discovering how seldom I listen is like suddenly discovering I am naked. Like Adam, I crouch and hide, not behind a fig leaf but behind rational reasons that seem to imply that a twentieth-century person cannot possess the same communion with God as a fourteenth-century monk. But deep from within comes the knowledge that no matter where I live, when I live, or how I live—I can still be awakened to God's presence. God does not depart from my daily routine. I am the one who closes my eyes, my ears, and the door.

This knowledge saddens me. I become impatient with myself. But then I think, *Perhaps my desire to listen for the still, small voice is a beginning.* It means I am conscious of what may be lacking. George Fox said, "He who shows a man his sin is the same that takes it away."[1] Until we find a hole, we are unable to fill it.

I think of a young infant, lying in his crib. He gives little thought to walking. But as he matures and grows, his desire to walk increases. I find I am like that child. I want very much to walk toward God. But even though I desire it, I am unskilled. I wobble and teeter. My back is stiff from falling. But God opens His arms and coaxes: "Keep trying, My child. Don't give up!"

So I persist. I try to listen for God despite the static in my life.

God Whispers When We Listen

I am reminded of a story of a man on his knees looking for something beneath a street light.

A passerby asks, "What are you looking for?"

"My glasses," the man responds.

Promptly, the passerby sets about helping the man look for his glasses. After he has looked for some time, he asks, "Are you sure you lost them here?"

"No," the man responds. He then points across the street. "I lost them over there."

"Then why are you looking for them here?" The passerby asks.

The man nods toward the street light. "Because the light is so much better here."

I often go about trying to hear God whisper "where the light is best." I listen for Him not where I lost Him (in my days crammed full of activity), but during my very rare "when" times. The light is always better during my "when" times: when I'm walking alone on a beach, when the house is quiet and empty, when I have nothing to do, when I find myself gazing at stars twinkling in the night sky.

I am discovering the reason I hear God better at my "when" times is because that is *when* I am listening. I have found that listening often means becoming conscious.

I remember one evening sitting on the deck with Mandy. Her arms and legs hung over the side of the glider as we rocked together in the coolness that comes only after the sun has set. We were quiet for a long time. I was mentally organizing all that had to be done the next day.

Mandy lifted her head from my chest and asked, "What's making that sound?"

I listened. "You mean the siren?" I asked.

She shook her head no.

I listened more closely. "Oh, maybe it's a radio or some children playing on the other side of the block."

"No," she insisted. "That other sound!"

That's when I heard the cicadas. Their song rose from the woods behind our house. Until that moment I had not even been aware of them.

In a similar way, we may be unconscious of God's whispers. Perhaps the static of sirens and radios and endless thoughts keep us from hearing Him. I believe God whispers in the midst of a business meeting, a traffic jam, a carpool, and a telephone conversation. And when we listen, *really listen,* we will hear God's whispers rising from the backdrop of all life, like the song of the cicadas.

God Whispers Right Where We Are

By "right where we are," I mean that God comes to us. Like the shepherd leaving the ninety-nine sheep to look for the lost lamb, God comes into our lives right where we are, whether it be in the kitchen, on the back porch, beside a grave, wherever His child is.

When I was five, I happened to be sitting on a wooden floor in the living room with my legs straddling a sheet of paper. It was there, I experienced my first whisper. I was coloring. Ever so often I looked up at the painting over the couch, and then I bent over my paper, trying to reproduce what my eyes saw—a picture of Christ praying in the garden of Gethsemane. Only then, I did not know much about Christ or Gethsemane.

As I drew with my crayon, I vividly remember thinking, *I can't believe it. This looks exactly like the painting!* I don't think the word *miracle* was in my vocabulary, but the "feeling of miracle" whispered in my mind, for I believed I had perfectly reproduced the painting on the wall. Surely my drawing was nothing more than a crude stick man. And the memory of my mother's words *that's very nice* support that. But something was greatly stirred within me.

I have pondered it often. What did it mean? I have come to believe that, in a primitive way, I encountered a whisper from God. My stick man was no ordinary man. But the miracle was not that I had drawn Him perfectly. The miracle was that I had stumbled upon perfection. God came to me right where I was. After thirty-three years the memory of it has not dimmed.

God has come to many people right where they are. He came to Norman Vincent Peale when his grandmother died. Peale wrote about standing beside his grandmother's grave. The minister, dressed in a coat with long, black tails, said of Jesus: "I am the resurrection, and the life: he that believeth in me, though he were dead, yet shall he live: And whosoever liveth and believeth in me shall never die:" (John 11:26).

Dr. Peale heard a whisper. He said his eyes were blinded suddenly by tears and his heart was warmed. "I had one of those deep intellectual and spiritual moments whereby certainty came into my mind—certainty without argument, without demonstration, without experiment. By intuition I knew the Scripture recited by that preacher was true, and I have tried to preach its truth through the years."[2]

God came to Norma Zankoski, right where she was—which happened to be in a pit of despair. Norma had lost both her parents to cancer in less than two years. Her grief imprisoned her. But one afternoon, God came to Norma right where she was and broke open the door to her prison. As Norma stared into the backyard, she noticed a cactus plant that she had almost thrown away many times. But that day, to her amazement, the cactus was ablaze with seven giant red blossoms.

Norma said her mind immediately filled with the words: "You view death as you have viewed this cactus, these many years—ugly, barren, and dry. Just as you could never have described or imagined the beauty of these blossoms before seeing them, you cannot begin to imagine or describe the beauty and the quality of life your parents have entered into with Me in eternity."

Norma said her heart flooded with peace, and she truly understood God's promise: "The joy of the Lord is your strength."[3]

These types of experiences speak to me. They say: God is not "out there" somewhere. God is with us every day in every activity. Like the cicada, He whispers, hoping His children will remember He is with them "alway."

Seek And Ye Shall Find

Our minister tells the story of two men walking in New York City.

One stops the other and says, "Do you hear that?"

"What?" the other asks, looking puzzled.

"That noise," says his friend. "I think it's coming from there." He points toward a drain pipe.

The other man hears only the buzz of traffic as cars and taxis disappear down Forty-Second Street.

By now his friend is on his knees, peering into the drain-pipe. "I think it's a cricket."

Sure enough the other man stoops and hears, "Creet, creet!" Both men sit for awhile listening to the cricket, unable to remember how long it has been since they have last done such a thing.

"Want to see something interesting," the older one says. "Nobody is paying attention to this cricket, right? Watch this." He fishes a quarter out of his pocket and throws it. The quarter clinks against the sidewalk and rolls a few feet away. Seven heads turn their way.

"See," he says. "You hear what you want to hear."

I thought about that for a long time: *"You hear what you want to hear."*

In my office, taped next to my desk is a quote from Henry Ford: "Whether you think you *can* or think you *can't*—you are right."[4] Could it be that hearing God whisper into our lives is that simple? If we think we can hear God whispering, and we want to hear Him, we will. Could it be as easy as "seek, and ye shall find"?

Jesus said yes. He said: "Ask, and it shall be given you; seek, and ye shall find; knock, and it shall be opened unto you" (Matt. 7:7).

He did not say, Seek, and maybe you will find. He did not say, Nine out of ten who seek, find. He said, Seek, and you will find. It is as if seeking, in and of itself, is a guarantee that we will find. What a tremendous promise!

Perhaps our search for God's whispers resembles that of the man tracing the sound of a cricket. As seekers, we must be willing to crawl on our knees and put our ears against a drain-pipe. But what happens when we lose our ability and desire to become seekers? When we become programmed to turn our heads only when quarters clink against the sidewalk? A sad story of an old mule comes to mind.

Hour after hour, day after day, year after year, a mule plodded in circles. He turned a millstone that ground grain. Eventually, the owner retired the mule to a lush pasture; he wanted to show his gratitude to the mule for many years of faithful service. He led the mule to the green pasture and released him. A brook beckoned beneath the shade of the oak trees. But the mule did not explore his new home. For the remainder of his life, he walked in a circle near the gate. He never became conscious of the beauty and freedom that were his.[5]

The image of the mule walking in circles haunts me. I keep thinking how sad that he never roamed the beautiful pasture around him. I cannot help but wonder if that mule and I have anything in common. Am I in God's beautiful, green pasture walking in circles, grinding some imaginary grain?

What about the times I leave the house, making all the routine turns, until suddenly I become conscious that I am taking the "store route" when I really wanted to go a different direction? What about the times Jim comes home from work, talks to me, gives me a hug and kiss, and goes upstairs to change his clothes, and I cannot even remember the color of his shirt or his tie?

My blind friend Helen said to me once. "Sometimes I get so aggravated when I ask someone to tell me what they saw, and they say, 'Oh, I didn't notice.' " She said, "If I could see, I believe I would notice everything!"

Hearing requires us to notice. Noticing requires us to become conscious. If we remain unconscious, we are robbed of an opportunity to explore the lush pasture of God's love. If, on the other hand, we break out of our routine ways of thinking and looking at things, if we reflect and listen, we will surely hear God whispering.

An example of this came to me one morning when I discovered an inch worm crawling up my sleeve. My first reaction was one of disgust. Immediately I raised my hand to knock the worm off my sleeve. Then something stopped me. I sat very still watching the celery-green worm. Stretch. Pull. Stop. Stretch. Pull. Stop. Tirelessly it moved, pulling an invisible wooden leg behind it.

I placed my finger in its path; it paused and then . . . stretch, pull, stop. It climbed onto my finger. It was the length of my smallest fingernail. I held it up to the sunlight, and its body became almost translucent, a moving ornament of colored crystal. For a long while it inched its way from one finger to another, its rhythm as relentless as the waves upon the sands.

Gently I lowered it onto a leaf, my disgust replaced with wonder. I have never left the sanctuary of a church feeling any closer to God than I did right at that moment. I had looked at a worm, *really* looked at it, and, in doing so, I heard God whisper that life, all life, is a miracle. I had become conscious. For a moment I glanced up and saw the pasture.

How about you? How often do you glance up and see the pasture? Perhaps we can search the pasture together so we might hear God whispering. Let's put our ears against a drainpipe. Let's kneel before the water pump, offer up our hands, and try to understand the meaning of the symbol being pressed into our palms. For, if we do, Christ promised: "Seek, and ye shall find" (Matt. 7:7).

Notes

1. George Fox, *Journal* (New York: Dutton, 1948), p. 35 quoted in Douglas Steere, *Together in Solitude* (New York: Crossroad Publishing, 1985), p. 139.

2. Norman Vincent Peale, "God's Answer Is Life," *Plus,* The Magazine of Positive Thinking, April 1987, p. 3.

3. Norma Zankoski, *The Upper Room,* Tuesday, 17 Feb. 1987, p. 54.

4. Quoted from *Foundations for Christian Living,* Feb. 1987, vol. 38, no. 1, Part 1, p. 12.

5. Patricia R. Garrison, *The Upper Room,* 3 July 1986, p. 7.

Earth is crammed with heaven,
And every common bush afire with God.

—Elizabeth Barrett Browning

3
God's Whispers Are Constant

If I look up from my routine and become conscious of living in God's pasture, I find it easier to hear God whispering. But if you were to ask, "Are you saying God whispers to you all the time?" I would have to answer yes and no. Yes I believe God whispers every day in every moment. But no I do not always hear Him. Yet my lack of hearing Him does not mean He is silent. It means only that I am not tuned in to the manner in which He speaks.

Thinking of God's whispers in the context of a seashell helps me. The seashell lays upon the sand, available to all who pass by. The sound of the ocean within the shell is constant—like God's presence. It does not become louder for one person and softer for another. It remains the same. The difference is whether we pass by the shell or whether we stop, put it against our ear, and listen. I believe it is the same with God.

He is available to each of His children. He is never far away. In fact, He is so close that we often have to step over Him to get to where we are going. Every experience, every form of creation holds the whisper of God within it like a seashell. A rose, a child, a cricket, a night sky, an old tom cat, cool flowing water—everything in creation bears witness to the God who created it. Do we draw these experiences close enough to hear the whisper of God arising from them? Is it possible to put these things against our inner ear, the soul, and hear God whispering?

I confess I do not hear God in all things. I wish I could. Perhaps that is my goal. If I were able to think about God as I went about my daily affairs, I would see Him more often in all things. Once again the necessary ingredient is becoming conscious. As a child, I had to learn that a seashell holds within it the ocean's whisper. As an adult, I am learning that all of life is a seashell, holding within it, the whisper of God.

God Knows Our Language

I believe God uses the language of our lives to speak to us. By language I don't mean French, English, or Spanish but the language of personal experience. This language is so personal and individual that God speaks differently to each one of us. He knows what brings a smile to my lips and to your lips. He knows what tugs at your heart and at mine. He knows your deepest need. He knows mine. He knows our thoughts, the special "little things" that bring depth and meaning into our relationships. He knows us more intimately than anyone else knows us. And He uses this intimacy just as we do in our own relationships.

"Heart-revealing intimacy," William Butler Yeats wrote in his poem "A Prayer for My Daughter."[1] Perhaps that is how God communicates, in heart-revealing intimacy. He knows us so well, and loves us so much, that He is able to whisper in ways that have meaning only for us.

Have you ever tried to describe a meaningful or moving experience to someone and been unable to adequately express how you felt? When this happens to me, I find myself saying, "Well, I guess you had to be there." The great thing about God is that He *is always* there. God knows about the little things of my life. He knows I love cats, walks by the ocean, and that precious hour before dusk. And knowing that, He uses them to whisper to me.

That type of communication is no different from the way we communicate with one another. We experience things together. Some things in our lives take on special meaning. And when that happens, in order to communicate with heart-revealing intimacy, we build upon those special moments. An example comes to mind.

Five months after our honeymoon, Jim and I moved from California to upstate New York where a job was waiting for Jim. He was to become a traveling auditor, a position that would require him to be away from home 60 percent of the time. On our way to New York, we had stopped at Yellowstone National Park to spend an evening in a cabin. I wanted so much to see a bear while we there, but it was October, and many of the bears had gone up into the hills. At lunch the next day, just before leaving the park and after looking for bears in vain, I pursed my lips in a mock pout and lamented, "I never saw my bear."

As we paid for our lunch at the cash register, Jim noticed a barrel of 49-cent bears about an inch high. He handed me one and said, "Here. Now, you've seen a bear!"

For whatever reason, we named the little bear Tonga. He traveled on the dashboard all the way to New York. And even after our arrival, Tonga appeared everywhere. I put him in Jim's medicine chest on top of his shaving cream. Jim hid him in a kitchen drawer. I tucked him inside Jim's pillowcase; Jim put him in my jewelry box. Our Tonga became a way of saying "I love you" to each other.

That is why I thought to tuck him inside Jim's suitcase as he packed for Brazil. The thought of being separated from my new husband for six weeks was almost more than

I could bear. Tonga was my way of going with him. Tonga carried my message of love. Jim said that night when he unpacked his clothes in a strange hotel room, the sight of Tonga nestled within his socks caused him to cry openly and without shame. Our 49-cent bear had said "I love you" on another continent.

By the world's standards Tonga is only a little thing. No insurance agent would understand the precious nature of my 49-cent bear! But God knows. He knows me intimately. He knows what a cat means to one child and a cactus to another. He uses these things to whisper with heart-revealing intimacy. He speaks our language. He says things in small little ways that are tremendously significant to us but merely coincidence to others.

I remember one morning worrying about an operation I was to undergo in several weeks. Black thoughts hung like clouds. What if something were to happen? At five years of age, how would Mandy cope with losing me? How would Jim manage to take care of her? I held my hands over my ears, actually hoping I could keep from hearing my own worries. In desperation, I asked for God's comfort.

No insight came. No words pressed themselves upon my mind. But a half hour later as I drove Mandy to preschool, I passed by a sign in front of a church. It said: "Why worry when you can pray?"

The only way I can describe the impact of seeing that sign, at that moment, is to compare it to finding Tonga nestled in my silverware drawer. Immediately, tears sprang to my eyes. It was as if I had been handed a seashell. And when I put it against my ear, I heard God whisper something that would help me face the days ahead: Instead of depleting my energy by worrying, I was to find peace through prayer.

That moment may seem as worthless as a dog-eared,

49-cent bear to someone else. But it was heart-revealing intimacy to me. For that reason, we cannot let others judge the worth of our whispers. No one can determine for us whether we have heard the ocean whispering from inside a shell. Hearing, feeling, and understanding are subjective. God's whispers are subjective. He speaks to us in personal, intimate ways that may, at times, hold meaning only for us.

Hearing God's Voice

I used to think that children were the most unconscious humans of all. They have little awareness of the world situation, famines, crime, and worries. But one day as I watched Mandy and her friend Lauren turning cart-wheels on the lawn, I discovered that I, not they, were unconscious.

While I had been watching the girls, I had been thinking about a talk I had given the week before and one that I was to give in several weeks. Over and over again, I played the tapes in my mind, oblivious to the glorious sunlight and cooling breeze. Most definitely, I plodded in circles unaware of the pasture that lay before me.

Mandy and Lauren, on the other hand, bathed themselves in the present moment. Worries about tomorrow or yesterday were like ghosts—ghosts they neither saw nor believed in! As they fell onto the grass, holding their stomachs and laughing, I once again realized why God wants us to be as little children. The two children before me were celebrating life, dancing to a music I seldom hear.

As I look around, I discover the constancy of God's presence. It seems God has waited on me so long. Only now am I beginning to recognize the many voices He used and still uses to whisper His love and presence. It seems that all of my life I have played hide-and-seek with

God, sometimes looking for Him, sometimes hiding from Him. As I recall a special tree from my childhood, I realize it was my favorite place to hide, and now I think, perhaps, it was God's favorite place to seek.

In the years before buying a Volkswagon van, Daddy somehow managed to squeeze a wife, six children, a wire-haired terrier, and luggage into a four-door, Ford sedan. Some twelve to fourteen hours later, with our car dragging bottom, the headlights revealed the dirt road that led to Grandpa's farm. By then most of my sisters were sleeping. But not me. Our annual trip to Halletsville, Texas, was my lifeline. I not only looked forward to visiting with my grandparents but also could not wait to climb up into my tree.

Through the years, that one giant oak, guarding the pasture had become my very best friend. Even now, the word *friend* does not describe adequately my feelings. Perhaps, sitting straddle legged across the lowest limb, my back pressing against the bark, I actually fell in love . . . with my tree. Knowing I could sit in its branches for two weeks made me strong enough to endure the painful days and nights of my childhood. But leaving it was always hard.

One good-bye stands out most in my mind. I was fifteen. I kicked clods on my way to the tree. It held out its arms as I climbed onto my favorite branch. The Spanish moss spilled from the limbs like tears. The wind whispered through the leaves. I looked up into the canopy before me where patches of sunlight chased away shadows. I had come, as a lover comes, for one last embrace.

Knowing that a year was too long to be separated, I painted the scene before me on the canvas of my mind. A white-petaled, wild flower peeked from the grasses. A black ant journeyed the hollows between the bark. A fly, cutting the silence, buzzed toward the barn. And a puff of wind lifted my bangs and stroked my face like a mother's fingertips. In the distance, the tin roof of the farmhouse glared like a mirror in the sun.

I thought I had captured all of it upon my mind. So whenever I wanted to, even though I was five hundred miles away and it was winter, I could turn into myself, where the painting was, and climb up into my tree. Even today that tree stands in my mind.

But the passing years have given me a keener sense of hearing. One day I shared with a friend that during my childhood I had gone to twelve schools, lived in thirteen states, and moved to more than twenty towns. I said: "You know, as a child, I always wanted roots."

Suddenly, the picture of my tree came back to me, and for the first time, I became conscious of its trunk where it sunk deep roots into the earth. I had had roots in the most literal sense of the word! What are "roots" except places where we have beginnings and from which we grow. The tree in my mind grounded me; it gave me a place to go to, a place that has moved with me wherever I have moved.

That discovery was like having God jump out from behind a curtain and yell "Boo!" Suddenly, I recognized His voice. He was in my painting, and I did not even know Him. Now I know how Cleopas felt as he walked on the road to Emmaus. He and his companion did not recognize Jesus when He joined them. They told Jesus how saddened they were about all that had happened to their mighty Teacher, Jesus of Nazareth. Jesus stayed with them, quoting passage after passage of Scripture. But it was not until Jesus sat down to eat and broke bread that they knew Him for who He was. Luke wrote: "Suddenly —it was as though their eyes were opened—they recognized him!" (24:31, TLB).

I am sure my success rate is poor. I have no idea how

many times I fail to recognize God's whispers as I step over the shells of my life. But I am learning God has many, many voices. I hear Him as I watch children turn cartwheels. I hear Him in an inch worm. I hear Him echoing from past memories. And whenever I hear him, I am always amazed. Yet I sense Him saying: "My child, why are you so surprised? I am here, I am always here."

The Moment of Looking Up

At one point in my life, when I was twenty-seven, I sat on my apartment porch reading a book. At the end of the book the writer said that if you have never done so, why don't you get down on your knees and turn your life over to Christ. I had never done this, so I knelt and said: "Lord, I don't exactly know how to turn my life over to You. But here I am."

Nothing came to me, no angels, no voices, no flashes of light. But a sense of peace passed through me. It's as if I had been relieved of a heavy load. Perhaps it was a feeling of doing cartwheels in the sunshine, in my Father's yard.

I see that moment as a turning point in my life. It's as if Christ came up to me, stopped me from going in circles, lifted my head, and showed me that I was standing in a beautiful pasture. He made me conscious of Him. He made me a better listener. He continues to help me recognize that God's whispers are found in every acre of earth, in every man, woman, and child, in every experience we will ever have. There is music in the world, God's music, and the pastures where we live are alive with it!

Note

1. William Butler Yeats, *The Norton Anthology of English Literature*, 3rd ed., vol. 2, (New York: W. W. Norton & Company, Inc., 1979), p. 1974.

The sacred moments, the moments of miracle, are often the everyday moments, the moments which, if we do not look with more than our eyes or listen with more than our ears, reveal only . . . the gardener, a stranger coming down the road behind us, a meal like any other meal. But if we look with our hearts, if we listen with all of our being and our imagination—if we live our lives not from vacation to vacation, from escape to escape, but from the miracle of one instant of our precious lives to the miracle of the next—what we may see is Jesus himself.

—Frederick Buechner

4
Listening for the Still, Small Voice

The still, small voice of God whispers within and whispers without. It is a quiet little voice, an inner knowing, a moment of adulation. It is the presence of God bubbling into my life like a fountain. Sometimes I wish I could hear it more clearly, as a shout instead of whisper, but then my faith and my free will might wither into nothingness. No, I think it better to discover the things in my life that act as little microphones—magnifying the still, small voice just enough to recognize the voice of my God.

In the Moment

Sometimes when the tic, tic, tic, of the clock fades into the background and I open myself to the moment before me, I hear the still, small voice. Time ceases to pass, no longer rushing past my ears. Rather, it pools in front of me. And I see within it the reflection of God. These pools are my sinking-in moments. They are the times I wade in the present, while the whispers of God lap about my ankles. One such moment was an evening when Mandy and I waded into the present to watch a mother robin and her birdlings.

I had just looked at my watch; it was Mandy's bedtime. But she was puzzling over the empty robin's nest that yesterday had held three birdlings. Gone were the chirping heads, bobbing about like cuckoos in a clock.

As we pondered the empty nest, the mother robin landed a few feet away with a wiggling worm in her mouth.
One of her birdlings popped up from the long grass,
spread his wings, signaling his whereabouts, and opened
his mouth. The robin hopped over to him and inserted her
beak into his. When she finished, the baby folded back
into the grass, out of sight.

Then Mom flew into a nearby thicket. That is when we
spotted her other two birdlings. They fussed and fretted,
cheeped and squawked, as they tried to balance themselves on a low limb. Suddenly, one of them fell off back-
wards. He let out an alarmed peep, fluttered his wings,
and thudded into the soft dirt below. He cheeped with
indignation as he rose to shake the dust from his down.
Clumsily he stood and shook himself so hard he fell side-
ways.

Mandy and I muffled our laughter. The mother robin
seemed beside herself. Her triplets were too old to remain
in the nest, but not quite ready to be on their own. It was
as if she had thought it would be easier—getting her off-
spring out of the nest and into the air.

I had never sympathized with a mother robin before.
But there, in the long shadows of evening, I did. And, in
doing so, both Mandy and I lost track of time. We waded
in the present moment. No other thoughts drifted upon
our island of consciousness—even though an hour of
world time had passed. I discovered that evening that
whenever I am plunged completely into the present moment I am driven closer to God.

It's as if God lives behind a giant pegboard, and the
holes in the pegboard are the everyday minutes of life.
Whenever I sink into a moment, I find a path to God.
Maybe that is what happened the morning the inch worm
climbed across my fingers. I followed it into one of the
holes in the pegboard and met God on the other side. And

when Mandy and I watched the robin, again, we sank into the moment, forgetting about time and counting time, and we touched something warm and wonderful.

I like to think that God's whispers come from these holes—that His still, small voice beckons us to discover His presence on the other side of every one of them.

Certainly the quiet reflective moments are great opportunities for us to "sink in." But if every moment is a hole, then every moment is a path to God. Even busy, boring ones! I have come to believe that if we allow it, any moment is more meaningful *if* we step into it below the surface level. I have even experienced a special moment while scouring stubborn stains on a broiler pan!

It was late summer and outside the kitchen window, Mandy sang to the sky on her swing. I envied her carefree afternoon, wondering how many of them I had experienced growing up. My mind paced like a caged tiger. It wanted free from my mundane chores!

So I opened the cage and let my mind out. I stood still and listened. The refrigerator hummed like a purring kitten. Mandy's song carried through the screen. The birds chirped to each other. The soft "pop" of bubbles floated from the metal sink, now glistening like polished pewter. Even the dishtowel took on a different look, becoming whiter, brighter. The sun slanted through the window, catching one of my soap bubbles and swirling it into a round rainbow.

This is the secret, I thought. Becoming aware of God in *every* moment. I think Paul knew this when he said we are to pray without ceasing. As we become more and more conscious, we hear God whispering all around us. By sinking into the moment, we tune out the static and become receptive to God's presence in our world.

In the Ordinary

Unfortunately, I sometimes wait for illness or death to plunge me into the depths where God's still, small voice can be heard. The day the space shuttle blew up I, like all of America, was stunned. I remember sitting down to write from that hollow place inside me. And what came from me was the realization that the threat of death often heightens our hearing and sensitivity—exposing the shallow and limited scope of *surface living.*

I wrote: It seems human existence is a delicate blend—very much here one minute and very much gone the next. It is unpredictable. In one second Christa McAuliffe and her colleagues crossed the threshold from life to death. They are somewhere else.

I find myself asking: If the crew members had their lives to live over again, would they do anything differently? Would their priorities change? If Christa knew she had only six more months to live, would she have given up the space mission? Would she have chosen long walks and more bedtime stories?

You and I do not know the exact hour of our deaths. It could be tomorrow, next month, or twenty years from now. Unfortunately, I tend to look farther down the road. For certainly, if I thought I were going to die tomorrow, I would go downstairs right this minute, take Mandy in my arms, and ineptly try to prepare her. I would look at her face as I have never looked at it before. I would hug Jim's neck as I have never hugged it before. But I gloss over these opportunities. I fail to hear the still, small voice whispering from them, for I believe there will be other opportunities tomorrow or the next day.

I remember reading about a woman who had been diagnosed to have an inoperable cancer. Later, she watched her young daughter eating peas. She described the experience as miraculous and beautiful—the way a small human hand could fold around a fork, delicately balance small green orbs, and lift them gracefully upward into a mouth. Life had become more precious. The mother did not see her daughter eating peas. Rather she saw HER DAUGHTER EATING PEAS! She heard the still, small voice whispering that life is truly miracle.

When does life cease being a miracle? When we stare out the window and see nothing? When senses become dulled with the dust of everyday living? When static drowns out the voice of God? Whatever it is, death shakes off the dust. It grabs you by the collar and pulls you so close you can smell its breath. And then suddenly, as you stare it in the face, you realize that you, too, could wake up some morning, eat breakfast, and die before lunch.

If I knew today were to be my last day here on earth, I would bathe in it, like a luxurious bubble bath. I, too, would see the miracle in a child eating a bowl of peas. No doubt, my whole being would come alive. My receptivity would be sharpened like the fine edge of a steel knife. Leaves rustling in the wind, the feel of Mandy's arms about my neck, Jim's rough, whiskered face—they would become gaping holes in my pegboard, leading me to the lap of God.

In the Bible

I have a letter written by John Carney to his wife in Sloansville, New York. The letter was written June 25, 1868. For his return address John wrote, "from My Old Post Under a tree." Evidently John was waiting to be released from the army; he wrote his wife "I should think you would begin to get discouraged, for I have wrote so many times I was a coming home and still I am here."

Either John or his wife was a relative of mine; the letter was given to me by my mother who found it in my grandmother's trunk. I have read this letter numerous times. Why? Because I want to know more about John, the way he lived, and his feelings. John probably never guessed that 120 years later, someone would be sitting in an office, complete with a word processor, smiling as she read his words: "I will eat the berries and write with ink." (John had written several lines of the letter with black raspberry juice.)

I treasure John's letter because it offers me one small slice of what life must have been like for those living in the 1800s. The letter was written three years after President Lincoln was assassinated and one year before the transcontinental railroad was completed. John's letter is a link to the past and my heritage.

In much the same way, the Bible is a link with those who came before us. It is rich with accounts of witnesses who saw and wrought miracles, men who were faithful to God, men who prophesied Christ's coming, and men who partook of the Lord's Last Supper. The Bible records covenants, prophecies, conversations, promises, and guidance. It carries within its pages, God's ageless message of love and salvation. It is God's love letter, His Living Word, capable of reaching across the centuries and touching the lives of all His children.

Time after time I have read of persons who, in their deepest moments of need, say a Bible verse suddenly surfaced in their thoughts. They may have learned the verse as many as fifty years earlier. But they remember it! And, in doing so, they are uplifted and filled with hope. God's words have a way of lodging within our subconscious and, when we desperately need to hear God's voice, springing forth like whispers from within.

Perhaps that is the power of the Bible. When we read it, we are given truth in the form of seeds. Even thousand-year-old seeds have germinated when planted in the proper soil. Perhaps, when we read the Bible, we are given these seeds, and, when the time is right, they germinate in our understanding. Only then do we discover the miracle of ancient seeds bringing forth tender shoots— even in our twentieth-century lives.

God set the cause-and-effect universe into motion. Even though time passes, customs change, and our knowledge increases, truth stands unchanged. The Bible remains the attempt of an all-knowing God to guide finite humans.

I have no trouble believing that the Bible is a guide to help us live our lives harmoniously within our cause-and-effect universe. I believe God realizes the dangers and perils of certain actions and behaviors. Perhaps, much of human folly is like that of a child wanting to play on a busy highway. Loving parents warn the child to stay away from busy highways. They issue this warning out of love, not tyranny.

But—even if we disobey and run onto the highway—I believe God still loves. I do not believe He lurks behind a steering wheel waiting to run over the child who dares to wander onto the highway. I do not believe He shrugs His shoulders and sighs: "I tried."

My God—the one I have learned to love—kneels and cries as He lifts broken, bleeding children from the pavement. He grieves because He loves.

This is the God I hear whispering from the pages of His living Word and every corner of the universe.

In Prayer

I believe Augustine said, "I find the more I have to do, the more I need to pray."

If I seek to hear God whispering in my busy world, I have found I desperately need to pray. Prayer draws me closer to God. In order to hear His whisper, I must draw close and become silent. Only then do God's warm, hushed words create a meaning in my mind. It's as if prayer is a magnet that draws me into proper alignment with God.

Thomas Kelly believed that prayer was an undercurrent of heavenly orientation, "as all the currents of our being set toward Him."[1] Prayer takes the focus from ourselves and directs it toward God. It helps us become still and receptive. Prayer is like the act of Helen Keller offering up her hand beneath the water pump. We are laid open.

Douglas Steere wrote that to pray "is to pay attention to the deepest thing that we know. . . . We are made awake: awake to our finitude, awake to the great gulf stream of love that will not let us go, awake to what each relationship in which we stand really means."[2]

To me, prayer reminds me of the cuddle times I have with Mandy. Our cuddle times—whether it be in early morning, when I put her down to sleep at night, or when she crawls into my lap to read a book—are intimate and special. These are usually our greatest moments of sharing. Sometimes she tells me how she feels. Sometimes I answer her questions. At other times we just sit quietly as we bask in one another's presence. These facets of a relationship can create intimacy with God as well as others.

I come to God in a myriad of ways. I come with my hurts, my confusion, my concerns, and my fears. I ask for God's guidance, His love, His comfort. I petition. I intercede. And occasionally, I sit with Him, basking in His presence, like I used to with my grandfather.

I still remember the times of hushed silence as Grandpa and I sat on the porch that circled the farmhouse. The hot, humid afternoons seemed made for staring out into the fields of cotton. Grandpa tilted his chair back. I twisted a strand of hair around one finger. If Grandma joined us, she fanned herself with one of her cardboard fans attached to a wooden stick.

Sometimes the silence was broken with a conversation concerning the size of tomatoes or a picnic that the church was planning. But it was the long silences between conversations that I most loved. It was the being there with the two of them that said more to me than words ever could.

I feel the same way about God. In the long silences of prayer, I truly hear Him. At those times, I become still and allow my soul—my inner ear—to turn itself toward God. In the whisper of love and communion, I hear my Creator speaking. I don't think it matters how I get onto God's porch, whether I climb the steps, hop up from the side, or open the door from inside the house. All that really matters is that I find God's porch and sit with Him.

If I seek His quiet voice, bubbling like a fountain, I will hear it better the nearer I draw to Him. That is why I attempt to crawl into the moments of my life, why I search for the miracle in the ordinary, why I seek His whispers in the Bible why I sit with Him in prayer. These are the little microphones of my existence which help me to hear a voice . . . whispering from within and without . . . that still, small voice of God.

Notes

1. Thomas Kelly, *A Testament of Devotion* (New York: Harper & Row Publishers, Inc., 1941), p. 44.
2. Douglas V. Steere, *Together in Solitude* (New York: The Crossroad Publishing Company, 1985), p. 23.

Never lose an opportunity to see anything beautiful.
Beauty is God's handwriting.

—Charles Kingsley

5
God Has Many Voices

Physically, I sat behind a steering wheel. Mentally, I frolicked across the fields like a long-legged colt. Fresh-scrubbed country air filled my nostrils and the breeze from the open window set my hair to dancing. Sunlight shimmered on the hood of my car, beautiful, bright sunlight. I felt like hugging the world. It seemed nothing could be more perfect.

Perhaps that is why tears filled my eyes when I came upon the field of wildflowers. An explosion of yellow overwhelmed my already aching soul. Acre after acre blazed with goldenrod. An army of flowers waved and applauded, giving praise to the morning and God. Maybe I should have felt foolish as tears splashed into my lap, but I did not. I felt only loved and thankful as the moment of rapture washed over me!

During such a moment, it seems impossible not to hear God whispering. Beauty reflects God's whispers . . . like sunlight on shiny chrome. But there are other times when God's whispers come to me, not as an army of blazing flowers but as a lone soldier.

Contrasted to my field of wildflowers is another moment. I sat in an ugly parking lot, feeling burdened and tired. *OK,* I challenged myself, *You believe God's fingerprints are everywhere, in every situation. Find one in this two-block square of asphalt!* Paper cups and mounds of emptied ashtrays littered the area. Truly, I could find nothing—until my eyes followed a crack in the blacktop where one wildflower stood like a lone soldier, saluting from a square inch of soil.

To me, that wild flower symbolized the touch of God. It said: *Even here, My fingerprint can be found! Perhaps, it is easier to find Me on a mountaintop or in a grassy meadow. But I am not limited. I can be found in less likely places. If you look, you can find Me whispering in every lonely, barren acre of life.*

I would guess that at one time or another we all find ourselves in a situation as bleak and ugly as a littered parking lot. I have searched many parking lots, and it's hard, hearing God whisper in such desolate surroundings. As I think back on my mother's life, I wonder if she ever found any wildflowers? And if she did, did she understand their significance? I know she saw none that day in early fall when she tried to end her life.

Maybe if I had answered yes right away instead of telling her I needed to take a walk and think about it, maybe it would not have happened.

But I did take a walk, out behind the bunkhouse, on the dirt road past the haystack. It was all part of a small Texas ranch. I had lived there once, for a year, after mother remarried for the third time. But now she was filing for yet another divorce. The tall grass beside the road stood lifeless, dry and brown. I felt older than eighteen.

Could I do what mother asked? Take my two younger sisters and raise them while she committed herself to a mental hospital? I knew she needed the help. I knew it a long time ago. Emotionally I felt I had always taken care of my younger sisters. But now, on my own, could I financially do it? My salary as a waitress was meager. And I didn't even have a place of my own. I was living, temporarily, with another family.

"What about sending the girls to live with Daddy?" I had asked.

Mom dropped her head. "I need something to live for," she whispered. "I don't want Les to take them away from me."

I searched the gray horizon. "Oh, God, what should I do?"

Walking back to the house, I knew what I would do. I would tell Mom I would take my sisters. When I opened the door to her bedroom, I saw her lying in two pools of blood.

I knew instantly what she had done. My sisters were playing in the other room with my grandmother who was recovering from a stroke. The lock was broken on the bedroom door, so I heaved Mom's dresser in front of it.

"Why?" I whispered angrily. "Why didn't you wait until I gave you my answer?"

She was pale and crying. I grabbed a sheet, ripped it into strips, and bound the two gashes on her wrists. We lived some miles outside a small town. After telephoning the doctor, I helped her to the car and drove straight to his office.

"Please, let her stay," Mom begged the doctor. He nodded his approval. He seemed to sense what I already knew. Mom needed me. She had always needed me. So I stood there, holding her bloody hand, willing myself not to faint, as the doctor sutured her wrist.

He shook his head and leaned forward, searching my mother's eyes. "Things can't be this bad can they?" He asked.

A tear rolled from my mother's cheek and dripped onto the white pillow case.

"Surely, God is more merciful than life," she whispered. "Peace. I just wanted peace."

Her white knuckles gripped my hand. I bent and kissed her forehead.

I do not know that Mom ever found peace on earth. But she did go on to live another ten years after that day. I am saddened by the fact her life was so painful for her. I wonder if my mother ever heard God whispering. Her words, "Surely God is more merciful than life," seemed to be saying that she did not hear God much in this world.

Perhaps she found herself in an ugly parking lot: three marriages ending in divorce, an addiction to sedatives, and the responsibility of six children. Perhaps her green pastures had been bulldozed over, coated with inch after inch of smothering, black asphalt.

I was part of that life. I lived in that parking lot too. But I guess I saw a crack, a place where the green pasture threatened to take back over some day, a place where the asphalt had broken and crumbled to reveal some soil, a place where a wildflower managed to grow. Instead of focusing on all the trash around me, I cupped my hand around the wildflower and sought its meaning. I must have come close enough to hear God whispering: "It is I. It is I."

Whenever stranded in the middle of despair and depression, I search for wildflowers—God's mercy and peace. Christ promised long ago, "I will not leave you comfortless: I will come to you." (John 14:18). And He does come. Over and over again. Sometimes He comes like a field of wildflowers spilling across the countryside; other times He comes like a lone soldier.

Whichever way He comes, we need only to recognize . . . and embrace Him.

Whispers in Nature

Nature seems to constantly put her finger to my lips and whisper, "Shhh, listen to what God is trying to tell you."

For that reason, I sometimes take my Bible with me to my favorite out-of-doors place. If you have never tried it, I recommend reading God's Word in the lap of the world He created. It can be a most meaningful experience.

I remember a morning in Lake Tahoe. I slipped out of bed before dawn. The cool air greeted me as as I quietly closed the door to our rented condominium. We were on vacation, and I did not want to waken Jim. Sinking my fingers deep into my sweater pockets, I walked barefoot across the cold sand toward the large boulders surrounded by water.

I found a hollowed place in one of the rocks and wiggled my body into a comfortable position. Reaching under my sweater, I pulled out my Bible and opened it to Genesis 1, the creation chapter. It seemed appropriate. Out across the lake bordered by blue lavender mountains, the light was being divided from the darkness. I read from the first page: "God saw the light, that it was good" (v. 4).

Ah, yes! So good! Morning had broken.

The sky was pink with the signature of dawn. The pine trees stepped forward from their shadows to be recognized, praising the sky with their branches. I read: "The earth brought forth grass, and herb yielding seed after his kind, and the tree yielding fruit, whose seed was in itself, after his kind: and God saw that it was good" (v. 12).

A duck rippled through the water, leaving a widening wake behind. A flock of geese honked on shore, signaling one another for flight. After a few flutters and splashes, the ten black-spotted geese passed before me in perfect v-formation, flying so low that their wing tips touched the water on each downward stroke. I stared after them, wondering. How did they know to go south?

A zoologist might tell me about instinct—that inborn tendency to behave in a certain way. But who gave a creature the ability to be printed with an inborn tendency to behave in a certain way? And I read: "God made the beast of the earth after his kind, and cattle after their kind, and every thing that creepeth upon the earth after his kind: and God saw that it was good." (v. 25).

I not only read about creation that day but also experienced it. Genesis came alive for me. I sensed what it must have been like—that first morning on earth. Whispered over and over again inside me were the words *"And God saw that it was good."*

This good is what Madeleine L'Engle referred to in her book *And It Was Good.* "All of creation is pattern,"wrote L'Engle,

> from the Great Dance of the galaxies to the equally Great Dance of the submicroscopic . . . Satan tried to make dissonances, to interrupt the rhythm, to distort the pattern. One of his most successful ploys is to make us believe that his distortions of the original good have destroyed that good. But they have not. It is only the distortions we must fear and shun, never the original good itself."[1]

Maybe that is why I recognize God's voice whispering through the pines. Maybe that is why I hear Him in the pink-hued morning and in the flight pattern of geese. Maybe that is why I am drawn to walk alone with Him on a beach. I hear God's whispers, spilling like wildflowers from the mountainsides of the original good. It is so much easier to hear God whispering when I experience the world as He intended it to be. That is why I think it is important to give myself an opportunity to appreciate it. And not just once a year on vacation!

I have discovered numerous ways to take "mini" vacations at home and still come away with feelings similar to those I experienced in Lake Tahoe, ways that put me in touch with the original good. I have tucked Mandy into bed, wrapped an afghan around me, and stretched out on my chaise lounge on the deck, looking up into the night sky. Star-gazing is a wonderful way to "tune in" to God. Sometimes I imagine I am a shepherd in Jesus' time. Other times I allow what I call my "star-gazing" verse of Scripture to sink in:

"When I look at the sky, which you have made,/at the moon and the stars,/which you set in their places—/what is man, that you think of him;/mere man, that you care for him?/Yet you made him inferior only to yourself,/you crowned him with glory and honor./You appointed him ruler over everything you made;/you placed him over all creation" (Ps. 8:3-6, GNB).

After an hour of star-gazing, I am changed. I feel closer to God, recreated with new life and freshness. Some years ago, I was surprised to learn that the word *recreation* actually means "a refreshing of strength or spirits after work or anxiety."[2] I used to think of recreation as only participating in a sport or hobby. But now I see it as any experience that gives new life or freshness, any experience that recreates us and puts us back in touch with the original good.

Getting up early enough to witness a sunrise, closing my eyes and listening to a tape of the ocean surf, eating a bowl of fresh strawberries and cream on the deck in early morning, cloud gazing, having a picnic under the sugar maple in the back yard, allowing the rays of the full moon to fall across my face, taking a walk at sunset—all of these things put me in touch with the original good that God created. I do not have to take a vacation in order to be recreated. I have to go no farther than my neighborhood. Every day, in countless ways, I can hear God whispering: *"And it was good."*

Using a Magnifying Glass

I remember carrying around a magnifying glass when I was a child. Through it a whole new dimension opened for me. Ants appeared the size of beetles. A tiny splinter turned into a log. The veins of a leaf became huge river beds winding their way across a rough, green field. My magnifying glass enabled me to see things in more detail —things I might have missed otherwise.

Perhaps my faith is a lot like my magnifying glass. When I focus my faith on anything—nature, people, or experiences—I discover a whole new dimension. I see things in more detail and I discover fingerprints—God's fingerprints—left on everything in creation.

Someone at Rebound, a Christian Rehabilitation Center in Charlotte, NC, is a master at using a magnifying glass. This person designed a brochure for a Christmas mailing. Pictured on the front of the brochure was an unshaven man, probably a wino. Beneath the picture, in big bold letters, were the words: THE SON OF GOD.

When the brochure arrived in the mail, I opened it and stared at the picture. I wondered. Was a wino the son of God?

I opened the brochure and read:

We are all sons and daughters of God. The meanest of us, the dirtiest, the saintliest, and the most humble. All God's children. And so he is our brother, the man who sips cheap wine and sleeps in doorways. And we are our brother's keeper. Christmas is coming. Our brother is cold. And hungry. And homeless. Who will warm him? And feed him? And shelter him? We will. With your help. Because he is the son of God. And he is our brother.

After reading the message inside, I flipped once again to the picture. I got out my magnifying glass and suddenly I recognized the wino. He *was* the son of God.

So it is when I hold up my magnifying glass. I am able to see something I have not seen before. The rude sales clerk, the man honking behind me at the stop light, the wino—they all carry within them a spark, a light, a whisper from God.

When One Person Reaches
Out to Another—God Whispers

If God is love and I believe He is, then every time one person reaches out to another, he paves a way for God. God is the love that flows between the two of them.

I remember a difficult evening some years ago. During dessert, a woman told me her husband cared for her too much to travel in his job. Her inference, since my husband traveled a great deal, was that my husband was less devoted to me. That innuendo struck a deep blow to my confidence. I had been married less than two years, and my husband had already traveled one and a half of those years. I was lonely. And I wished, more than anything, that my husband did come home every night for dinner.

I tried to hide my hurt from the woman and my other friends who were there. Later, with little enthusiasm, I said good night, walked to my apartment, and unlocked the door. I surveyed the living room. The cold television set, the empty chairs, the neatly folded afghan—everything was just as I had left it—untouched.

Somehow the living room reflected my mood: untouched and unloved. Jim was hundreds of miles away. And God? *Probably even farther,* I reasoned. After all, He was busy with the "heavy" stuff. With everything going on in the world, did He *really* care that I was lonely? I had enough food to eat; I was healthy; I had family and friends. I concluded I had no right to bother God with my feelings. So, I braced myself for a long, lonely night.

About twenty minutes later, close to midnight, the

doorbell rang. I looked out the peephole and saw my friend Diana who lived in the same apartment building. She had been at the coffee too. I opened the door.

"Here," she said, carrying one long-stemmed red rose. "I thought you could use this. Rick sent me a dozen for our anniversary."

With that, she smiled and left.

To this day, I do not think Diana realized what her rose meant to me. I turned back to the living room. The television set, the chairs, the neatly folded afghan—they did not look the same anymore. The fragrance of Diana's rose filled the room. Something else filled the room too, something created when one person reaches out to another. It is the essence of God. It is love.

God cares. Even in a hurting world, God cares about the small things that matter to us. I know God cares because I care. Even though a child dies every minute from hunger, I care that Mandy has fallen. I bend in love and stick a bandage on her knee. Jesus said: "If ye then, being evil, know how to give good gifts unto your children, how much more shall your Father which is in heaven give good things to them that ask him?" (Matt. 7:11).

God does not weigh one request against another. He is not limited. He cares about all things at once. His presence can fit into the smallest request, the simplest gesture, the nearest hand. God has many voices—including that of people. He dwells within each of us. That part of Himself, within us, touches and warms the heart of another.

Hold Fast to the Whispers

In one letter to the Thessalonians, Paul wrote: "Examine everything carefully; hold fast to that which is good" (1 Thess. 5:21, NASB).

I remember being in a store with Mandy and turning

around to find she was not there. My heart began to pound as I searched in every direction. My knees went weak. What if someone had taken her? We were in the mall where two previous attempts had been made to take small children.

I readied myself to start screaming. That's when I saw her—peeking out from under a clothes rack, a tag dangling across her nose as she looked up and smiled. Relief flooded my body. She scampered to her feet and came running into my arms. I remember the feeling of closing my arms around her. I believe, in that moment, I held fast to that which was good.

As we experience the world around us, we are to *hold fast* or treasure those wonderful moments and insights that God whispers our way. We are to *hold fast* to the beauty, the goodness, and the love we encounter. When we stumble upon a field of wildflowers, a sunrise, or a friend bearing a rose, we are to hold fast—because the goodness within them unfolds into a whisper from God.

Notes

1. Madeleine L'Engle, *And It Was Good,* (Wheaton, Ill.: Harold Shaw Publishers, 1983), P. 192.

2. The *New Merriam-Webster Pocket Dictionary,* (New York: Pocket Books, a division of Simon & Schuster, Inc., 1971).

To every thing there is a season, and a time to every purpose under the heaven.

—Ecclesiastes 3:1

6
Timing and God's Whispers

On the shelf in my office is a "Precious Moments" figurine—a girl, dressed in a cap and gown, holding a diploma in her hand. Jim gave it to me when I was thirty and enrolled at Ohio State University. At that time in my life, I was bullied by doubt. I had so many questions: What did I hope to accomplish by going back to school? What did the kids in the classroom, ten years my junior, think about me? Was I ready to cope with grades, midterms, and papers at this stage in my life?

All these things weighed in the back of my mind as I studied for a Spanish test, an exam that would be given orally and individually. The professor planned to grade us on our ability to understand and converse with him one on one in Spanish. The thought was about as appealing as the plate of cooked celery my Aunt Mildred used to scoot in front of me when I was a young child.

Sighing, I conjugated again the Spanish verb *escribir* meaning "to write." Just then Jim walked into my office and set a package in my lap. "Happy Birthday," he announced.

I peeled the paper from the box, lifted the lid, and unwound the tissue. Inside, I found the outward expression of my inward desire—a female graduate. Jim smiled, seeming to sense he had found the perfect gift. Little did he know his timing also was perfect. For my graduate seeming to sense he had found the perfect gift. Little did he know his timing also was perfect. For my graduate shrunk my iceberg of doubt into a small ice cube. The words *You can do it!* formed in my mind when I looked at her.

A few days later, with sweaty palms, I sat before the Spanish professor and *hablo espanol.* I practically skipped out of his office. I knew I had done well! If Jim had been there, I would have given him the biggest hug. I appreciated his love and support and the fact that he had given me a perfect gift when I needed it most. It was an affirmation of his love and concern.

Jim touched me when I most needed it. His timing made the gift of the graduate all the more special. Perfect timing turns the ordinary into the extraordinary. Perfect timing is receiving an unexpected check that covers a worrisome debt. Perfect timing is walking back through the house one more time before leaving, only to discover a burner still on under a pan. Perfect timing is a friend handing you a rose at the moment you have decided you are unloved.

We all possess a certain ability to sense when the time is right for certain words or actions. When I love someone, when I am close to another, when I see fear or depression welling up within others, I know it is time to whisper my love and concern. Surely, my God, who is far greater than I, can sense these very things. If I know how to do these things, won't God sense even more certainly when the time is right? Doesn't His ability far exceed my own?

Only God knows a person's innermost thoughts. He sees what lies beyond tomorrow. He perceives the latent potential hidden within us. He, more than anyone, knows how to turn the ordinary into the extraordinary through timing. Timing transforms a glass of water into miracle. For someone, whose tongue swells from thirst as he staggers across the scorching sand, a glass of water—at that precise moment—is a miracle.

I'm convinced God creates minimiracles in our lives all the time, but we fail to notice them or pass them off as coincidences. Just yesterday, I was talking with a friend whose daughter, Jane, is unmarried and pregnant. Jane is nineteen. She is considering adoption. The attorney, who would be handling the adoption, gave Jane, without names, the biographies of three families who wanted to adopt a child. He wanted to know which one Jane would pick. Jane read the biographies, and one woman stood out in her mind.

Later, the attorney called and said, "A funny thing happened right after you left my office." He said one of the women, whose biography he had given Jane, called and said, "I know you'll probably think this is crazy, and I haven't talked to you in so long, but I just felt an urge to call and see if maybe you might have a baby for us." The woman was the same woman Jane had decided would be the "right" mother!

Jane said, "Isn't that a coincidence, Mom?" My wise friend said, "Some people would call it coincidence. But we have been praying for the best family for your child. I think this is God's answer."

Some people call these happenings coincidences. I like to think of them as God's whispers, tailor made, to fit the unique shape of our experiences.

God's Care or Coincidence?

William Temple wrote, "When I pray coincidences happen and when I do not—they don't."[1] Things in my life seem to unfold much the same way. If I am seeking answers and guidance, I believe patterns and meanings emerge from my everyday routine. I am reminded again of Helen Keller kneeling at the water pump with her

teacher Anne. It was not coincidence that Anne spelled
w-a-t-e-r in Helen's palm as the water flowed over Helen's
hand. It was Anne's attempt to stretch Helen's mind to
the limits of understanding.

I believe God, too, attempts to stretch us to the limits
of understanding. Oliver Wendell Holmes said, "Every
now and then a man's mind is stretched by a new idea and
never shrinks back to its original proportions."[2] Once we
become aware of God's attempts to communicate with us,
our consciousness is stretched to the point it will never
again shrink back to its original state. If we become conscious of the timing of events in our lives, we may discover, like many others, that God uses this timing to speak to
us, even in small ways.

I remember one morning when this happened during
my morning prayer, before I began to write. Even though
I was running short on time, I flipped open my Bible to
Nehemiah. I did not remember much about the biblical
character Nehemiah; quite frankly, at that moment, I was
not all that interested to refresh my memory. But I had
a feeling I was *supposed* to read that chapter.

I read a few verses and thought: *This is silly! I'm not
getting a thing out of this chapter, and here I'm reading
it because I think I'm "supposed" to.* I almost closed the
Bible. But I still felt the nudging, the whisper to go ahead
and read it.

OK, I'll read it, I thought. *But I don't know why.*

Not more than fifteen minutes later the telephone rang
and it was my friend Helen.

"Terry, do you have time to listen to my article, I just
finished it this morning?" she asked. "I thought I'd do a
little something different this month. It's about Nehemiah."

I started laughing. "So you're the reason I had to read
Nehemiah this morning!"

The more I follow my nudgings, the more often this sort
of thing happens. God has ways of letting us know we are

on the right track, that we are within His will. And I believe timing is one of the ways He reaffirms us in that knowledge.

Not too long ago I read a story about Marta Gabre-Tsadick, who lived in Ethiopia. After Ethiopia's Emperor Haile Selassie died, Marta, who was a government loyalist, and her family found it necessary to flee for their lives. For some reason, just before getting into the Land-Rover that was to drive them to safety, Marta ran back into her house. *What am I doing?* she wondered. She looked around, picked up a roll of adhesive tape and a jar of Vaseline, and stuffed them into her purse.

Later, in their perilous drive across bush terrain, the tape was used to repair the top of their Land-rover to keep out the cold night air.

And the jar of Vaseline?

One morning, after the wheel bearings had been ground to powder from the pounding journey, Marta's husband folded strips of aluminum foil and fit them into the wheel. He turned to Marta and said. "Marta, we need grease. Do you have any cosmetics? Any cold cream?"

Marta said, "I reached into my purse and held up the jar of Vaseline—the jar the Lord had prompted me to retrieve as we left."[3]

Coincidence? I don't think so. God's faithful care? I believe so. Marta listened to the whisper within her, the prompting to grab a roll of tape and a jar of Vaseline. It was God's timing that turned them into tools for their escape. God turns ordinary things into answered prayer and minimiracles. But the only reason something extraordinary happens is because of the timing—the fact that it came to us in our *exact* hour of need. We need only to become conscious of the many ways and times God whispers to us through timing. Maybe we, too, will discover that prayer and seeming coincidences walk hand in hand.

Unconnected Circumstances, Part of God's Timing

Someone once suggested I do a time line of my life. I offer it as a suggestion to help you see if the unconnected circumstances of your life weave some sort of pattern. Starting at birth, write, in chronological order, the many changes that have taken place in your life. Following a straight line, on a long sheet of paper plot the highs and lows and what you consider to be your spiritual turning points.

Charting my time line allowed me to step back and look at my life from another vantage point. In doing so, events no longer seemed like a random string of coincidences. I began to see the influence of circumstances and others upon me, how moving from one place to another promoted both my professional and spiritual growth, and how events and friendships seemed to come at just the "right" time.

Some things, like my interest in writing, come together like steps on a ladder, one experience leading to another. And my walk with God seems closer and closer as the years stretch out before me. And yet not everything falls together or makes sense. I have some question marks. But I am beginning to view my experiences like bits and pieces of material sewn together in such a way as to make a quilt. God is the master quilt maker. He has patterns more intricate and beautiful than I have ever even dreamed or imagined.

God has given us free wills. But He is the maestro of the universe. His rhythm and timing guide us and attempt to bring us into harmony within Himself.

God's Timing Affirms

In my book *Forgive Me, Lord, I Goofed!,* I wrote about

a time I felt God used timing to affirm my actions. I would like to share that story with you.

I left the wallpaper store trying to decide if the bathroom really needed to be wallpapered. The paper cost more than I thought it would but the soft coral print was so pretty. I just could not make up my mind.

On my way to the car, I remembered I needed to get two boxes of plastic sheets for my files. Some people cannot resist bakeries or candy shops. I cannot resist the lure of an office supply or stationery store.

I fingered the notebooks, flipped through the files, and checked the prices on the big boxes of envelopes. When I got to the cash register, my arms held much more than the two boxes of plastic sheets I had come in for. There were paper clips, a new file basket, a big roll of labels, a flip file for my addresses, pencils, and some typing paper.

When the clerk rang up the bill, I thought it sounded a bit low, but I paid him what he asked and took my bag to the car. There I opened it and compared my purchases with the cash register receipt. Just as I suspected. The clerk had undercharged me; he had only rung up one box of plastic sheets instead of two.

What a deal! The sheets cost eleven dollars a box. I got two for the price of one.

I drove home feeling good about the error made in my favor. Of course, had the error been to my disadvantage, I would have gone back. But after rationalizing the situation, I figured there were plenty of times I had been shortchanged at the grocery or department stores and probably never even noticed.

It all works out in the end, I told myself.

As I put away the things in my office, I came upon a story I had mailed to the editor of a Sunday School magazine. A nagging feeling pulled at me. I wrote about God, love, truth, and kindness.

What had I done one hour earlier? Rubbed my greedy

hands together and delighted in the fact that I had received something for nothing.

I knew I would have to make amends. The store had already closed. But the next morning, as soon as the store opened, I handed my receipt to the clerk.

"Hi. I came in yesterday and bought two boxes of your plastic sheets for ringed binders."

"Yes?"

"Well, you only charged me for one box."

"Excuse me?" he said incredulously.

I was sure he heard what I said, but I repeated it just the same.

"Yesterday, I bought two boxes of these plastic sheets, and you only charged me for one."

He shook his head. "Just a minute, I need to go talk to the manager."

I overheard him saying something about "a lady who says we undercharged her."

The manager eyed me carefully. They continued to talk, and then the clerk came back.

"Well, I guess you owe us eleven dollars then. Thank you for coming back. It is a little unusual though."

I did not want to bask too long in his praise or tell him of my initial reaction. I paid the eleven dollars and went outside feeling much happier.

I was so happy, in fact, that I decided to go next door to the wallpaper store and buy that wallpaper for the bathroom. When I told the lady what I wanted, she said, "Well, today must be your lucky day! We just reduced that paper this morning. It's 30 percent off!"[4]

Coincidence? I don't think so. The timing was too much in step with my inner struggle and growth. The wallpaper being reduced one day and not the next was an affirmation—much like the ones I give to Mandy after she has had to retrace her steps by apologizing or making amends.

Sometimes, I feel as though I have a teacher. Could it be the same teacher Jesus speaks of in John's Gospel? "The Helper, the Holy Spirit, whom the Father will send in my name, will teach you everything and make you remember all that I have told you" (John 14:26, GNB).

It certainly seems like I have a Teacher. I have noticed how one book reinforces another. How sometimes, when I walk through the library or a book store, the perfect book seems to find its way into my hands. How, when I read a verse in the Old Testament and haphazardly flip to a verse in the New Testament, it refers to the verse I just read. I think this is God's way of guiding and teaching me. "Seek, and ye shall find," He promised (Matt. 7:7).

In one day, I encountered three affirmations about "shining our light" into the world. Early one morning I read an article about the importance of shining our light into a dark world and how it helps others see. That afternoon, I met a lady in a store who, during our conversation, pointed up to the sky and said, "Just let your light shine." That evening I called a friend in another state, only to have her tell me about a great sermon her pastor preached about letting your light shine. From that experience I paused to ponder and reflect: How might I more effectively "shine *my* light."

I do not know how many people experience things coming in threes like that, but I do know, from conversations with others, I am not alone in this matter. Sometimes, certain words, thoughts, or Scriptures make a greater impact upon me than normal. If these incidents happened only once, I might chalk it up to coincidence. But when they happen again and again, I believe I am being gently guided. Another example comes to mind.

Several years ago, I struggled with the decision to set aside time for morning prayer and devotion. How vital was it to my spiritual growth? Within a month, my question was answered. I subscribe to *Reader's Digest, Guide-posts,* and *The Christian Writer,* and all three magazines, within a span of four weeks, contained articles expounding on the importance of morning devotion. I took the hint.

When I encounter my *affirmation of threes,* I become very moved. The thought of God *actually* reaching into my existence and touching my life is extraordinary. But my affirmations are not everyday occurences. They are more rare, like rainbows or four-leaf clovers or a child falling asleep in my arms.

Sometimes I wonder, *Is it possible to become more alert to these whispers of guidance and affirmation?* Maybe the secret is in training. Astronomers, because they have been trained, see planetary positions, the location of galaxies, and can names of various suns in the night sky. Fishermen, because they have been trained, see clues in the shadows and ripples beneath the waters of a lake. Photographers, because they have been trained, develop keen eyes for lighting and composition.

Training often determines what we see and hear. Perhaps I can train myself to listen for God's whispers in the world around me by sinking deeper into His presence. Christ came to help. He can stretch us until we will never again shrink back to our original size. Christ can sharpen our hearing. He can magnify the whispers, lingering within in the shadow of every living thing and experience.

If we possess faith, desire, an ongoing awareness, and ask God to guide us, I believe we will hear God whispering into our lives. It may take a while to learn His language. We may have to struggle, as I did to learn Spanish. But just as there is a Spanish word for everything I encounter, there is also a God-word. The God-word whispers in the sunrise, in a wild flower, in a cat, in a friend bearing a rose, and in the timing . . . of their touch.

Notes

1. William Temple, *Love Gift,* Perry Tanksley, ed. (Old Tappan, N.J.: Fleming H. Revell Co., 1971), p. 30.

2. Oliver Wendell Holmes, quoted in ibid., p. 38.

3. Marta Gabre-Tsadick, "Fleeing for Our Lives," *Guideposts,* July 1987, pp. 28-31.

4. Terry Helwig, *Forgive Me, Lord, I Goofed!* (Nashville: Broadman Press, 1986), pp. 95-97.

If you do not understand my silence;
you will not understand my words.

7
When God Is Silent

I have a friend who says she believes in the holiness of everything . . . even rust on a fence. I, too, believe in the holiness of all things. And when I see this holiness, I hear God whispering. Yet, there have been times when this holiness has become unrecognizable.

In the long, dark halls of silence, holiness dims. As I pass through these halls, I become nearsighted and deaf. As I grope for answers, I have had to ask myself, *Does my deafness mean God is mute?*

I do not think so. The world doesn't change when persons lose their hearing. Bells still clang. Birds continue to sing. Children carry on with their laughter. The loss of hearing means only that one individual's ears no longer interpret the vibration of these sounds. Deaf persons know this. Out of necessity, they develop other means of *hearing.* They depend upon other signs to compensate for their loss.

When I cannot hear God, I also must compensate. I believe my greatest compensation is my faith, faith that believes in God and never falters—even when I feel frightened and alone; faith like that of the psalmist who wrote: "Yea, though I walk through the valley of the shadow of death, I will fear no evil: for thou art with me" (Ps. 23:4).

Perhaps, more than anything else, the story of a twelve-

year-old girl has inspired me to trust in my God, even in
my moments of deafness.

During a caving expedition, a twelve-year-old child
became separated from her group. She lost her way in one
of the dark passages and never again answered the cries
of her friends. Rescue workers were called in, and days
passed. The girl was found too late. Her lifeless form lay
huddled against the corner of a deep, dark cave. But the
faith of that child never wavered. Scrawled on the cave
wall beside her were the words: "I believe in the sun even
when it isn't shining; I believe in God, even when He is
silent."[1]

This message came from a child swallowed by darkness.
But in the darkness a beacon flashed. It was the undying
faith of a twelve-year-old. I, too, want this beacon within
me. A beacon that shines in the day, in the night, in the
calm, and most especially in the storm.

I will do everything in my power to hear God whispering into the world. I will look for His holiness in all things.
But when I fail to see and hear, may I never *fail to believe!*

The Cruelest Lies Are Often Told in Silence

Robert Louis Stevenson may have meant something
else when he wrote, "The cruelest lies are often told in
silence,"[2] but his words describe precisely what happens
when I am met with silence. I begin to doubt. I start
asking myself: *Have I done something wrong? Am I being
punished? Is there a problem with the way I'm praying?*

It's as if the tempter hisses: "You silly creature! You
can't *really* communicate with God. So, why all the fuss?"

I have had to stop and ask myself: *Why do I make a
fuss? Why am I bothered by silence?*

I know why. I am like a child crying in the night. When
I cry out to my Father and He does not answer, I feel
abandoned. The poignant words: "My God, my God, why

hast thou forsaken me?" (Mark 15:34) echo through my being.

Perhaps that is why the words of the twelve-year-old warm me so. She seemed to know that God's silence had nothing to do with His presence or absence. It's as if she seemed to understand that God is with us always whether we feel Him or hear Him. Our *feelings* of forsakenness are only illusions, lies whispered into the darkness.

Imagine the lie of the first winter. Leaves were stripped off the trees for the first time. The flowers died. The grasses turned brown. Birds flew away and animals went into hiding, as the cold winds coughed out a blanket of white death. The land lay dead and forsaken, killed by winter. But then something happened. Spring came. And it turned out that the lie was not that winter came. The lie was that winter endured forever.

So it is in our lives. The lie is not that we will have feelings of silence or forsakenness, because we most surely will. The lie is that they will endure forever. God has not promised us a life of ecstatic communion here on earth. But He has promised never to abandon us. The Bible is filled with promises of His presence. He has given us something to hold onto when we are lowered into the vacuum of silence. God has also given humans the ability to believe in things not seen.

When winter comes, I know it will not last forever. I know that lying dormant, within the earth, are seeds and bulbs and roots, patiently waiting for spring. My silences are only periods of dormancy. If I realize this, I can cling to the promise of spring, and the promise will see me through.

Weathering the Winter of Silence

Frederick Buechner said that God is our beloved enemy because He demands of us everything—our lives, our selves, our wills, and our treasure. But when we offer up everything to God, we experience resurrection. Like Jesus of Nazareth staggering on broken feet out of the tomb toward the resurrection, we experience the magnificent defeat of the human soul—at the hands of God.[3]

Within the depths of our silences, we may experience this magnificent defeat to which Buechner refers. I believe we emerge from these defeats new creatures, like the phoenix raised from its own ashes. My awakening or spiritual growth spurts are usually preceded by a time of unrest, doubt, and silence. It's as if I am being stretched, and stretching is often painful. It seems I pass through seasons. I have my springs of new awareness, my summers of warm communion, my autumns of unrest, and my winters of cold silence.

Faith gets me through my winters. Faith tells me the warmth and joy of summer will return. Faith says all seasons will pass. Like the writer of Ecclesiastes, I have come to understand that all life has cycles and seasons. "To every thing there is a season, and a time to every purpose under the heaven: A time to be born, and a time to die, . . . a time to keep silence, and a time to speak" (3:1-7).

Perhaps the secret to contentment lies in my ability to weather all seasons—even the seasons of doubt and silence. I have a great fondness for trees. Year after year, season after season, they have an incredible ability to weather the elements. They are remarkable symbols of strength and endurance. I am especially fond of our sugar maple growing in the backyard. We planted it some fifteen feet from the deck, in hopes that we could someday sit beneath a canopy of leaves. Every summer I measure its growth. I count how many boards of the deck are now covered by its shade. To my delight, the number has increased through the years, as the shade creeps closer and closer to my glider.

If I sink my roots deep into a faith based on God's love, my growth can parallel that of the sugar maple. During the long summers of my communion, I can grow and blossom. During the winter, I can tap those roots for nourishment that will see me through until spring. If I expect silence in my life, if I prepare for it, and if I know it is only temporary, surely I will survive it with my faith intact.

I like to think that God measures my growth the way I measure the sugar maple's. I pray that, inch by inch, the shade of my faith is creeping closer and closer toward Him.

The Other Side of Silence

Have you ever noticed that life seems to be a bundle of paradoxes? Birth is actually death from the womb. Death is birth into the hereafter. Jesus died so we might live.

All paradoxes seem to be separated by a thin curtain. And, depending on what side of the curtain we stand, our perception will be different. When someone walks from the kitchen into the dining room, it can be perceived in two ways. If I am in the kitchen, I see the act as leaving. But if I am in the dining room, I see the very same act as coming.

Not long ago I read *The Velveteen Rabbit* by Margery William to Mandy. While reading it, I loved the way Williams took what many of us might consider ugly and revealed instead the great beauty within. It is paradox at its loveliest.

In a nursery scene, an old rocking horse, the Skin Horse, befriends a rather new and unsure Rabbit. Their conversation follows:

The Skin Horse had lived in the nursery longer than any of the others. He was so old that his brown coat was bald in patches and showed the seams underneath, and most of the hairs in his tail had been pulled out to string bead necklaces. He was wise, for he had seen a long succession of mechanical toys arrive to boast and swagger, and by-and-by break their mainsprings and pass away. He knew that they were only toys and would never turn into anything else. For nursery magic is very strange and wonderful, and only those playthings that are old and wise and experienced like the Skin Horse understand all about it.

"What is REAL?" asked the Rabbit one day. "Does it mean having things that buzz inside you and a stick-out handle?"

"Real isn't how you are made," said the Skin Horse. "It's a thing that happens to you. When a child loves you for a long, long time, not just to play with, but REALLY loves you, then you become Real."

"Does it hurt?"

"Sometimes," [said the Skin Horse] for he was always truthful. "When you are Real you don't mind being hurt."

"Does it happen all at once, like being wound up, or bit by bit."

"It doesn't happen all at once. You become. It takes a long time. That's why it doesn't often happen to people who break easily, or who have sharp edges, or who have to be carefully kept. Generally, by the time you are Real, most of your hair has been loved off, and your eyes drop out and you get loose in the joints and very shabby.

"But these things don't matter at all, because once you are Real you can't be ugly, except to people who don't understand."[4]

When I go into Mandy's bedroom and see her dolls—dirty, torn, and worn—I know Margery was right. Mandy loves these dolls; somehow in loving them, they are real. She has other dolls on the shelves, with perfect curls, but they have been untouched and unloved. Most of them don't even have names. They aren't real.

The paradox of the nursery magic is that the Rabbit will become more beautiful as he grows more worn.

Then, if ugliness is really beauty, and leaving can be entering, and dying is birth into another existence, isn't it possible that silence might even be hearing? Perhaps, on another level, our soul hears best in silence. Perhaps silence is a time of preparation, a time of gathering before breaking forth, a time of rest.

As much as Mandy dislikes it when I send her to her room for "rest time," I know it is a time she needs to regenerate. She feels as though I am shutting her out, but I am actually embracing her need to rest. What if the same is true with God? What if in the long halls of silence, He is embracing my need? Could it be that what I perceive to be negative is actually positive?

Perhaps, the story of the Skin Horse has something to say to all of us. In order to become REAL, a conscious child of God, we may be asked to endure long silences that hold no meaning for us. The process may hurt sometimes. And it may not happen all at once. We may have to become. And it may take a long time. Maybe that is why becoming REAL doesn't happen to people who break easily, who have sharp edges, or who have to be carefully kept. Maybe, by the time we become REAL, most of our hair will be loved off, our eyes will drop out, and we will be loose in the joints and very shabby. But these things don't matter at all because once we are REAL we can't be ugly, except to people who don't understand.

This is the thread that I hang onto when I think about the ultimate silence experienced by a twelve-year-old girl dying in a cave. You see, I picture Christ saying to her, "This thing that has happened to your body doesn't matter at all because you are REAL, a child of God. And once you are REAL, you can't die, except to people who don't understand."

Making Peace with Silence

I used to get depressed every fall. Even if the weather was beautiful and the trees were afire with color, a sadness overshadowed me. For me, the turning leaves announced the coming of winter. And I never liked winter. Even as a young child, I remember asking my mother, "Why does winter have to come? Why can't we have summer all year long?"

Mom said winter made summer more precious. It seems my mother had made peace with winter. Through the years, I have learned to make peace too. I have come to love toasting marshmallows over a cozy, warm fire in the fireplace. I now cherish the cold that forces me to seek good books and warm afghans. I even look forward to the first snow so Mandy and I can build a snowman and throw snowballs at each other. I have learned to love my enemy. I have made peace with winter.

In the same way, I am learning to make peace with the silences of my life. I no longer view silence as an enemy. It is only a season, a rhythm of my humanity. All of my life I have moved to this rhythm, like the swinging pendulum of a clock. The back and forth, the up and down, the coming and the going, the in and the out—they are breaths of creation. I do not know why silence comes; I only know that it does.

It comes, like winter, forcing me to seek the flame of God . . . burning from within. For that reason I have made peace with silence. It is an enemy turned friend.

Notes

1. Mrs. Major Howard Chase, "When the Sun Doesn't Shine." *The War Cry,* 19 May 1986, p. 7.
2. Robert Louis Stevenson, quoted in John Bartlett, *Bartlett's Familiar Quotations,* 15th ed. (Boston: Little Brown and Company, 1980), p. 667.
3. Frederick Buechner, *The Magnificent Defeat* (San Francisco: Harper and Row, 1966), p. 18.
4. Margery Williams, *The Velveteen Rabbit* (New York: Alfred A. Knopf, 1985) as adapted by Mark Sottnick for the video version of *The Velveteen Rabbit,* narrated by Meryl Streep.

The wind of God is always blowing . . .
but you must hoist your sail

—Fenelon

8
Obeying God's Whispers

At one time or another, I think we all shrug off or ignore whispers from God. I know I have. I get impressions or feelings I should do something, but I run the idea through the logical, left side of my brain, and it says: *Nah, forget it. It doesn't make any sense."*

Remember my Nehemiah story? That incident is not of great consequence—except it suggests to me that my moments of intuition may actually be whispers from God. Isn't it possible that God gave us intuitive capabilities so we might be more receptive to Him? If we believe in the presence of a soul within us and the presence of the Holy Spirit in our world, is it difficult to believe God communicates to us through feelings, impressions and circumstances?

I believe God sometimes whispers by bringing an impression of feeling into our conscious minds. We are given an idea, a warning, or a confirmation. But, as with all God's gifts, we are also given a choice to accept or refuse what we have been given. Very seldom does God force-feed us. He allows us the choice of belief or unbelief, trust or suspicion. Obedience or rebellion.

My suspicious nature, my logical side, my left brain— whatever you want to call it—is not very obedient. Sometimes, it shakes its head, stamps its foot, and demands to know *who, what, when, where,* and *why.* It bullies. It

103

rushes toward my intuitive butterflies, grabs them by the wings, and stuffs them into its pockets. It tries to hide and discredit whatever gifts intuition bears.

I am not suggesting that left-brain function is inferior. Absolutely not. But neither is it supreme. My intuitive nature is as critical to my growth and development as my logical nature. And if I want to hear God whispering into my world, I think I need to trust that inner voice—without making it a prisoner of logic.

But if my intuition and impressions do not make logical sense, what should I do? Am I to be obedient, even if I do not understand? I think each of us has to find the answer to that question for ourselves. I think of Abraham believing that Sarah was pregnant even after childbearing age. I think of Noah, sweating beneath the sun, as he built a monstrous ark. I think of Moses walking toward the Red Sea, as he watched the dust of chariots rising behind him. I think of Peter straddling the boat, looking into the water and then again at his Master.

I remember a morning some years ago when I was impressed with the thought, *You better lock up the house today.* My pat reply to this was, *"That's silly!"* And it did seem silly. In all the years of growing up, we had never locked the house, and nothing had ever happened. The possibility that anything would be different that day did not make any sense to me. My intuition locked horns with my logical nature and lost. I left the door unlocked. That afternoon, I returned to find the door ajar. We had been robbed! I remember thinking, *If only I had listened.*

I believe we humans *hear* these whispers, but we don't really *listen* to them. Instead of obeying, we often club them back into a hole, denying ourselves the experience of divine guidance.

Logic May Impair Hearing

If I shrug off what I hear and refuse to act on it, I may silence God's whispers. If I insist on using logic as a measure for what I have heard, I can choke the miracle right out of a situation. Miracles seem to happen to people who trust and obey. Over the years, I have subscribed to a little inspirational magazine. I would like to recount, four stories from it which illustrate perfectly our need to obey rather than question.

The first story is about a man, E. S., who came to grips with his alcoholism. He joined a group dedicated to helping people achieve sobriety. At one of his group meetings, the landlady of a hotel, in a section of town known as Wino Gulch, called for help.

E. S. and another man volunteered. At the hotel, the landlady led them into a squalid room where a grizzled oldster lay in a stupor on the bed. E. S.'s partner, a veteran at such visits, patiently talked to the semiconscious form. He explained that he himself had once been a drunk. But that, by turning his life and will over to a higher power, he had gained both sobriety and serenity.

"I'm leaving my card," his partner said. "I'd like you to attend a meeting at this address."

As they left, E. S. commented, "*That* was a waste of time."

"You never know," was his partner's only reply.

At their next meeting, a shaky but sober young man came up to E. S. and his partner. "Thank you for coming to Wino Gulch that night," he said. "You saved my life."

They stared in astonishment. Obviously, the young man was *not* the man they had talked to in the hotel.

"That's right," the young man replied, holding out the card they had left. "But I heard every word you said. I was *under* the bed."[1]

E. S. and his partner had no way of knowing that young man was under the bed. And while it may not have seemed logical to go on talking to a semiconscious man, E. S.'s partner felt compelled to do so. Only through obedience to that inner whisper was another man's life saved.

In another story, a woman was working as a waitress at a restaurant. She had to work late one night and debated whether she should try to catch a ride home or walk. Deciding that a ride would cost too much, she prayed for her safety, wrapped some leftover chicken to take home with her, and stepped into the dark street.

Within moments a man came up behind her, put a knife to her throat, and whispered: "Just wait till I get you home."

She prayed for God to help her. Then she said she "heard" the words *eat your chicken.*

The thought horrified her. With the cold blade of a knife pressed against her throat, she was supposed to eat her chicken? To her, the message defied logic. But again came the impression *eat your chicken.*

She started crying as she unwrapped her chicken and brought a piece to her mouth. She knew she could not eat, but she tried. Just then, from the alley, she heard noises, like that of dogs. Evidently hungry and smelling the chicken, they aggressively raced toward her and the attacker. Her attacker became scared and ran away.[2]

As hard as it is to believe, that woman probably saved her life by eating her chicken. If that had been me, I doubt I would have been as obedient. If I heard the words *eat your chicken,* I would think my mind was suffering from some kind of shock or trauma. What is logical about eating chicken when someone has a knife to your throat? Nothing I guess—unless a Power higher than ourselves knows of two large, hungry dogs foraging for food in a nearby alley.

The third example comes from Marion Bond West's article "God Does Speak to Us." Marion believed that God's voice is gentle, never pushy—even in dangerous situations. She wrote of a time God spoke to her, when her boys were young, as she stood frying chicken for supper. She said she kept "hearing," in a calm voice, *Go find your boys. Now.*"

Finally, with her hands still covered in flour, she went to look for her two sons. She thought, *How silly to stop cooking just to look for the boys.*" That's when she found Jon and Jeremy in the washroom. Jeremy was crouched in the dryer with the door shut, wearing a space helmet. Jon was about to blast him off into outer space by pushing the "On" button.[3]

Even though she "felt silly," Marion heeded the whisper. No doubt, she saved her son from injury, possibly even death.

The last story I would like to share is about Eros and Bartie Savage. They set out in their cabin cruiser for a picnic dinner on south San Francisco Bay. On the way, they waved to a college crew team heading out for a practice row.

When the couple neared the San Mateo Bridge, the water had turned into large choppy waves. The bridge tender refused to lift the bridge, pointing to the white-caps on the water ahead of them. So the couple turned to go home. In the distance, they saw a ruby-red light in the shape of a cross glowing near the mud flats.

Mesmerized, they turned their craft in that direction. Eros felt irresponsible because he knew the engine could suck up mud in the shallow water and be ruined. But he felt *compelled* to follow the cross. Even when mud

spewed from the exhaust pipe and the engine tempera-
ture rose into the danger zone, they kept going.

When they came closer, they discovered the light was
only a buoy reflecting the sunset. They felt very foolish;
they had actually risked their boat to chase a mirage.

That's when Bartie noticed coconuts floating in the water. Then, to her horror, she realized they weren't coconuts; they were heads of men! The men from the rowing
crew had crashed into the bridge, and their boat had sunk.
They had been in the water for over an hour. Facing
death, gulping the icy salt water, they had come to a point
of desperation and had prayed together for rescue.

God chose the nearest hands. And, despite the fact it
seemed illogical, Eros and Bartie obeyed.

If any of these individuals had relied only on logic, no
transformation, no rescue, no miracle would have taken
place. It appears that understanding very often *succeeds*
obedience. I try to remember that when I feel led or
guided. I try to step out in faith and trust that my Heavenly Father will honor my obedience.

Stepping Out in Faith Requires Action

Stepping out in faith requires some action. As crazy as
this may sound, I used to walk my cat, Tigs, on a leash. Tigs
was a fourteen-pound cat with a somewhat antisocial per-
sonality who was less than thrilled with the idea of walking. I shouldn't say that. She liked the first three minutes.
She ran down the apartment steps, raced out the door
toward the yard, and started to nibble on the grass. That
was her favorite part and probably the only reason she
ever agreed to walk in the first place.

After she chomped on a few blades, I would tug her
leash, signaling that it was time to go on. Rarely was our
walk a continuous flow of motion. We had lots of starts and
stops. Mostly stops. Finally, when Tigs could tolerate me

no longer, she would flop to her side and become rag-doll limp. No amount of coaxing, pushing, or prodding could get her to stand upright again. Whenever that happened, I lifted my fourteen-pound fur ball from the sidewalk and carried her back into the apartment. Our *walk* was over.

Trying to walk an uncooperative cat is nearly impossible. Trying to guide an inert individual can be almost as difficult. I have always heard it is easier to change the course of an object if it is in motion. If something is in motion, it takes a lot less force to change the course than if the object is still.

Perhaps it is the same with people who are striving to do God's will. We may have to be in motion. If I am praying about a situation, I try to move forward trusting that what is happening *is* God's will. If a door slams shut, I look for windows. I know of few instances in the Bible where persons obeyed God by sitting passively waiting for platters to deliver them to heaven.

This reminds me of a joke. It seems a man, trying to escape flood waters, climbed on top of his roof. As the water rose, the man prayed, "Lord, please rescue me."

Not long after, a man in a boat stopped and asked, "Can I help you?"

"No thanks," the man on the roof answered. "I'm praying to God, and I have complete trust in Him. He will rescue me."

A short time later, a helicopter hovered overhead, and the pilot lowered a rope ladder.

The man on the roof waved him off and shouted, "Thanks. But I'm praying, and God is going to save me."

Eventually the man drowned and went to heaven. When he saw God, he asked in disbelief, "What happened? I trusted that You would save me, and I ended up drowning."

God replied, "I tried. But you refused the boat and helicopter I sent for you!"

If I am trying to be obedient to God's will, I feel I have to move forward, take the opportunities that present themselves, and trust that God is whispering through those opportunities. If a feeling tugs inside me, I realize I may be called into some sort of action. The question is: Will I be obedient to that call? Peter was. He stood and lifted his foot over the side of the boat. The waitress in the story was obedient; she unwrapped her chicken. Marion Bond West chose obedience. She stopped cooking and went in search of her boys.

All of them—Peter, the waitress, and Marion—obeyed by stepping out in faith. It seems God cannot catch us *until* we obey His whisper to step out in faith, thereby falling into His arms of grace.

Obedience Is the Opposite of Apathy

I have often prayed for solutions to my problems. But someone asked me once if I had ever prayed that I would *be* a solution to a problem? Wait a minute! That means getting involved, taking some action, and crawling out of my warm, comfortable blanket of apathy. I think that is exactly what God intends for us to do. If we are His hands, if we carry within us the whisper of God for someone else, I believe God is calling us into action. He wants us to obey that nagging little voice that whispers: When you have done it to the least of these, you have done it unto Me (Matt. 25:40).

I remember an afternoon that brought me face-to-face with a choice. Mandy and I were driving past a store when a dog ran in front of our car. He looked pathetic. He slinked forward like he had a fifty-pound rock strapped to his back. His sides caved where his stomach was. His tail curled between his legs, and his head hung low, as if he were ashamed of his condition.

My heart ached for him as I watched him crawl beneath a bush beside a store that sold popcorn.

"What's wrong with that dog?" Mandy wanted to know. "He looks sad."

I debated what to do. "He's a stray, Honey. He probably doesn't have a home." I paused. "Why don't we say a little prayer for him?"

As concerned-sounding words fell from my mouth, I remembered the words of James: "Suppose there are brothers or sisters who need clothes and don't have enough to eat. What good is there in your saying to them, 'God bless you! Keep warm and eat well!'—if you don't give them the necessities of life?" (Jas. 2:15-16, GNB).

My prayer, too, sounded empty. Why should I leave it to someone else to help the dog? Perhaps I was supposed to *be* that someone. I felt a nudge, I heard a whisper, urging me into action. I looked at Mandy, realizing I wanted her to grow up with a sense of responsibility to help others. I did not want to set an example of apathy, merely flopping over on my side, turning my head, and expecting that someone else would do whatever needed to be done. Apathy is not being obedient to God's whispers—it is ignoring them.

I groaned a little when this realization hit me. It meant I would have to invest some time, some caring. It meant I might not get everything on my "to do" list done. It meant I would have to stop and help the dog.

"What are you doing?" Mandy asked as I swerved into a fast-food parking lot.

"We're going to order a hamburger and some water for the dog. I can tell he's really hungry."

As we walked across the street and tried to coax the dog out from beneath the bushes, I watched my daughter gingerly break the hamburger into bite-sized pieces. We both talked to the dog; he came out, ever so slowly, toward us. He gulped down the hamburger, drank the water, gave us a look that seemed grateful for our small act of kindness, and crawled back beneath the bush. Meanwhile, we went inside a nearby store and called the animal patrol. The dog would be rescued. Mandy and I prayed for the dog for almost a week after that, and, somehow, our prayers no longer sounded empty. Maybe it was because we had obeyed that small voice whispering from within.

You see, I think obeying God's whispers and stepping out in faith very often mean we will be led to others in need. Obedience is not the easiest path; it requires action, maybe even sacrifice. Christ's path of obedience led Him all the way to the cross. Certainly, obedience leads us past the roadblocks of logic, past the hills of apathy, and into the land of becoming . . . becoming closer to, and evermore conscious of, a whispering God in our world.

Notes

1. E. S., "His Mysterious Ways," *Guideposts Magazine,* May 1985.

2. *Guideposts Magazine,* Sept. 1985.

3. Marion Bond West, *Guideposts Magazine,* "God Does Speak To Us," by Marion Bond West, June 1986.

I sought my soul—
but my soul I could not see;
I sought my God—
but my God eluded me;
I sought my brother—
and found all three.

—William Blake

9
Misunderstanding God's Whispers

It seems appropriate that this chapter should follow the chapter on obeying God's whispers. I often wonder if what I *think* I hear is actually God whispering. How can I be sure I am not misunderstanding God's whispers? The truth is I can never be absolutely sure. Whispering is tricky. It has a greater margin for error and misinterpretation. Unless I were to have an unmistakable Damascus experience like Paul (which I have never had), I run the risk of misunderstanding what God is whispering.

By the very act of becoming receptive, I open myself to the ugly and evil as well as the beautiful and good. I hear not only the birds singing but also sirens screaming. I hear hurtful words, words of prejudice, and words of the tempter. Madeleine L'engle said we pay a price for our vision. So, too, do I believe we pay a price for our hearing. We run the risk of misunderstanding what we hear.

Since we are human, we will either misunderstand or we will come into contact with someone else who has misunderstood. We are like prospectors looking for gold—in our zeal to find it, we may be fooled by fool's gold. Fool's gold is anything that resembles good but requires us to compromise our integrity.

Satan whispered to Jesus. He offered Jesus the very thing He came to die for—mankind. From a high mountain, Satan pointed to all the kingdoms of the world, "All

115

this I will give you, if you kneel down and worship me."
Satan was offering to surrender without a fight. But
. . . Jesus would have to disobey God in order to gain it.
He turned and said, "Go away, Satan! The scripture says,
'Worship the Lord your God and serve only him!' " (Matt.
4:10, GNB). Jesus would not compromise.

For Jesus to accept what Satan was offering would have
been like going against the grain of the universe. And
when we go against the grain of the universe, we get
splinters in our soul.[1] Whenever we go in the opposite
direction of the highest good for all concerned, we are apt
to get splinters in our soul.

Whispers from God are pristine. They run *with* the
grain of the universe He created. They are truth blazing
a trail through the darkness. They gather, they reconcile,
they mend, they spill over with love. When I hear a whisper, I need to ask myself, *Would anyone be hurt by this?
Do I have to step on anyone to reach this goal? Am I going
against the grain of the universe to achieve it? Am I serv-
ing only God and no one else?*

These questions are the best sieve I have to strain out
misunderstanding. Yet, I realize, even they are not fool-
proof. I am human. I am finite. I am fallible. How can I
even expect to interpret the whispers of an omnipotent
God, who is like an ocean while I am but a cracked teacup,
unable to hold any more of God than my brim will allow.

Perhaps that is why we are instructed to be meek and
humble. These two virtues remind me over and over
again how fallible I am as a human. I am to forget about
the splinter in my brother's eye and concentrate on the
log in my own. If I make the mistake of believing I am
infallible, that I have all the answers, that I *know exactly*
what God wants for you, I become proud and haughty and
sure instead of meek, humble, and needful.

I have encountered well-meaning individuals who

seem to believe they have all the answers within their cracked teacups. They have shoved open the door to my life and trampled their muddy footprints across my beliefs. They have sent crashing to the floor the shelf of my soul that held my crystal whispers of truth and communion. They tell me this is God's will. I look up to God and ask, Have they only misunderstood?

To See Ourselves as Others See Us

If we proclaim we have a direct line to God, free from any human interference, we may turn people off to God instead of on. In my own profession of writing, some individuals seem to believe that they are infallible when it comes to hearing God. Several editor friends of mine have received letters from writers saying, basically, that God dictated their manuscripts.

One of the letters read: *You must publish this and don't change a word. I have been divinely inspired. And God told me to tell you to publish it.* This was only one of many such letters this editor had received. She answered that in all probability God would not make spelling errors and grammatical mistakes. But if God told *her* (the editor) to publish the manuscript, the woman could rest assured she would.

Another letter read: *I have chosen you to publish Our book. If you do publish my book—you will receive rivers of blessing from Heaven but if you do not you will see my wrath saith the Lord. The choice is yours saith the Lord.*

These letters frighten me. I am a writer. I believe God gives me insight into what I write. But I find it difficult to believe (maybe because it has never happened to me) that God dictates word for word what someone puts down on paper. To me, that's the easy way out. It means not going to the library for research, no rewriting, no looking up how to spell words in the dictionary, no soul-searching for just the right phrase. It also means believing one is infallible when it comes to interpreting God's whispers.

How can any one of us say we are above human fallibility? I most certainly cannot. Listening for God whisper into my life does not mean I know all the answers. It does not mean I am free of misunderstanding. It does not mean that every idea that pops into my head is God given. Listening for God's whispers means only that I am trying, the best way I know, to open myself to God's presence in the world.

I have a difficult time hearing God whisper through the rigid individuals who wave letters in front of my face, proclaiming they have *all* the answers! It is meek individuals, who confess they do not know all the answers, who speak most loudly to me of God. I hear God whispering through their humility. I see God shining through the windows of their souls. Somehow, by admitting they may misunderstand what God is saying, they comfort me. It is as though the meek individual says to me: "We are *both* cracked tea-cups, my friend. But, come, let us dip together in the same ocean of love."

Notes

1. Tottie Ellis, "Keep checkbook open; they need the money," *USA Today*, 27 Mar. 1987, p. 12A, an opposing view.

Who has not found the heaven below
  Will fail of it above.
God's residence is next to mine,
  His furniture is love.

—Emily Dickinson

10
Whispers of Love

A guest speaker shared with me, and others in the audience, her search to hear God whispering in her life. She said it took courage because she feared God would be displeased. She pictured Him shaking His finger and reminding her of the many ways she had failed Him. But after much soul searching, she decided to stop running and brace herself for whatever it was God had to say. So she removed her armor and laid herself open. Day after day, she waited in her downstairs office.

Finally, one morning, she heard God whispering. And His message broke her heart. She had prepared for God's wrath, His disapproval, His punishment—everything *except* His love. When God finally spoke, He embraced her with the words: *You are my beloved.* He did not belittle or berate. He did not condemn. He only loved.

You are my beloved.

I cannot speak for you, but I know I respond best to whispers of love. When I am loved and accepted, I am free to become the best I can be. Love throws open the windows to God's divine light. Thomas Kelly said that the light of divine presence helps us "to respond, in some increased measure, in ways dimly suggestive of the Son of Man."[1] Love kindles that part of me, made in the image of God. Love bonds, awakening in me the great need I have to love back.

Returning God's Whispers of Love

That afternoon, long ago, on the porch of my apartment, when I offered Christ the reins to my life, I experienced a sense of peace. But, for several years thereafter, my heart and my head played tug-of-war. It seemed my head said, *You are supposed to love God, and God is supposed to love you.* But my heart argued, *Why can't I FEEL that love?*

I remember praying, "Please, God, teach me to love You." Then I held my breath, half expecting a lightning bolt to strike the edge of the bed. Admitting I did not love God was an ugly confession, almost blasphemous it seemed to me. Maybe I was being selfish. But I longed for what the book in my hands described as an "intimate relationship" with my Heavenly Father.

Faith was not enough. I wanted more. I wanted love, the kind of love that would permeate my whole being, the kind of love that could pierce my heart with a shaft of light. I was no longer satisfied with my long-distance relationship—heaven to earth—God ruling on high while I muddled through below. I *knew* God's arms were around me, but I wanted to *feel* them. I wanted my head knowledge translated into a language my heart could understand.

There were moments in my life, brief ones, when I did understand. Once I had felt an overpowering, overflowing love for my Creator. I was a child, swinging into the blue sky one afternoon. The sun blinded my eyes and warmed my face. My hair tickled my cheeks while the rhythm of the swing tickled my insides. I stretched my feet higher into the air, and suddenly my heart soared out of my body and hurled itself toward God. I was suspended in a glorious moment of love and adoration. It was a magic moment, but a fragile one. It sadly disappeared. The next day, hard as I tried, I could not get the swing to go high enough to feel that way again.

I put the book on my bedside table and turned my face into the night to talk with God. "Are You so great, so mighty, so big, that my heart is too small for You? Am I to be content with head knowledge instead of heartfelt emotion? I yearn for a love that surpasses my love for all others!"

No answers came to me that night. No angels. No visions. No whispers. Deep down I wondered if I were asking for the wrong thing. Was the feeling I sought a kind of puppy-love experience too immature to even ask for? I wrestled most of the night with that question and eventually gave into sleep.

Somehow my prayer found its way to the attic of my mind. There it gathered dust and lay forgotten like a musty, one-eyed teddy bear. It remained there until another teddy bear came into my life, a soft blue one that Jim bought for our newborn daughter. It sat in the corner of her crib, watching over her in the night.

As moonlight spilled through the ruffled curtains of the nursery, I saw the blue teddy bear in the shadows, patiently waiting for his charge. Porcelain light bathed his fur as well as the face of my sleeping child. Even though Mandy slept, I held her. I soaked up the wonder and miracle of her. I listened to her breathing. I felt the warmth and weight of her in my arms. My love spilled across her like the moonlight.

As we rocked in the quiet shadows, I became aware of someone else in my thoughts. Someone very near. Someone very loving. Someone who whispered into my heart: *My child this is how I love you. You are this cherished, this treasured, this loved, this miraculous. Even though you sleep, I hold you. I have always loved you. My love spills across your life, like the moonlight on your daughter's face.*

I remembered the prayer I had cast aside. Then the width and depth of my love for God poured forth and streamed down my cheeks. I lifted my face to Him. He who is great and mighty and big. And my heart received a beautiful translation from my mind: *I love You, too, Father. With all my heart, all my soul, and all my mind.*

God's Whispers of Love Transform

I confess the rapture of that moment faded. But the memory of it has not. Falling *in love* with God changed me. I began praying more. I started listening for God's whispers. My writing took a new direction—toward Him. More than anything, I wanted to love God back. Since that night in the nursery, I have experienced other moments when that same *love-light* rushes through me with such force that tears come—the kind of tears that spill when too much joy has been stuffed in, and you feel as if you might burst wide open into a thousand particles of happiness.

I am unable to create those moments for myself. They are gifts, given without warning, shooting through my existence like falling stars. All I can do is keep a watchful eye for them and recognize the light when it falls across my face. Annie Dillard said, "I cannot cause light; the most I can do is try to put myself in the path of its beam."[2]

I can try to put myself in the path of God's beam. Perhaps that is where I can best hear His whispers. But where, in the world of overpopulation, AIDS, war, and cold-blooded crimes, do I find God's light? I think the answer lies within each of us. God's light can be found in our expression of love and compassion. Wherever an individual bears the light of love, the darkness is lifted.

You see, it takes very little light to brighten a dark

world. I remember someone giving an example of this. He said to picture a stadium of fifty thousand people, sitting in total darkness. No one can see. There is *only* darkness. But if one person in that stadium lights a candle, all fifty thousand people would be able to share in that light . . . the darkness would be broken.

Two thousand years ago, the darkness was broken. A child came into the world, carrying God's beaming light within Him. The Gospel writer John said that God loved the world so much that He gave us His only begotten Son. "For God did not send his Son into the world to be its judge, but to be its Savior" (John 3:17, GNB). I believe Christ is God's greatest whisper of love. Christ is the Light that shines. And love is the passing of His light from one to another in a darkened world.

When God Whispers, "I Love You," There Is Harmony Within

In explaining his relationship with God, an introspective person commented, "I believe people vibrate at a higher frequency whenever they connect with God." I like that image.

I sometimes picture myself as a bell. Whenever God whispers "I love you," I am set to ringing with the force of His love. His music and notes have perfect pitch, perfect harmony. Only when my hands hinder the bell does it thud with muffled clanks. In the hands of God, I vibrate with His crystal clear notes of love.

I believe we all have a bell within us. When we hear God whispering His love, this bell sets to ringing in harmony with the universe. God's whispers are gifts—given randomly—sometimes when we least expect them. But, whenever I find myself in the path of God's beaming love, harmony and peace ring throughout my being.

I pray that you, too, have had moments when the bell

was held just right—when the notes and music resonated throughout creation, in a glorious moment of communion —a moment when you heard God whisper, *My dear, precious child, you are, indeed, my beloved.*

Notes

1. Thomas Kelly, *A Testament of Devotion* (New York: Harper & Row Publishers, 1941), p. 44.
2. Annie Dillard, *Pilgrim at Tinker Creek,* (New York: Harper & Row, 1974), p. 33.

The place where man vitally finds God . .
is within his own experience
of goodness, truth and beauty.

127

11
No Longer Will I ask

How many times have I looked into my brother's face and failed to see the Christ in him staring back at me? How many times have I failed to see the fingerprint of God pressed upon my life? How many times have I sat in darkness with a match in one hand and a candle in the other? I don't know the answers to these questions. I don't think anyone does. But understanding often seems so simple in hindsight. I slap my forehead and say, "Of course!"

I wonder if Helen Keller ever asked herself how many times Anne Sullivan had tried to communicate with her before she finally understood. When patches of confusion rearrange themselves to create understanding, an incredible step has been taken. A person is made awake and, like Rip Van Winkle, made conscious of something always there but never realized. The giant step from unconsciousness into consciousness can be as life changing as learning to communicate for the first time. Or as remarkable as seeing Christ where nothing was seen before.

You see, I believe life camouflages God. Being unconscious of God does not negate Him. I may have brushed against Him thousands of times in my life and not recognized Him. But, even if I do not recognize or hear Him, I believe He is here . . . patiently waiting for me to catch a glimpse of something mysterious, something beautiful, something which instantly causes His presence to jump out at me. And *Presto!* I am conscious of a whispering God—the same God who has always been here, camouflaged within the scenes of my life.

I do not know the scope of all I have missed or will continue to miss. But I am thankful to the people who have tapped me on the shoulder, pointed to a God I could not see, and traced His image until I found Him. Their vision started me on my journey. Their vision caused me to bend, pick up my shell of faith, and listen for the still, small voice of God. Because of them, I understand that God has always been whispering.

No longer will I ask my Lord, When did You speak to me? When did You hug me? When did You whisper? For I am sure His answers would encompass *all* of my life. I picture Him saying:

Remember your grandfather's tree? It was then I hugged you.

Remember your cat Boots? It was then I cried with you.

Remember the flower in the parking lot? It was then I offered you hope.

Remember the morning on the lake, with the Canadian geese? It was then I felt your joy, beating within My own heart.

My friend, may the presence, the peace, and the love of God the Father, be whispered into every moment of your life. Amen.